PUTTING MORALITY BACK INTO POLITICS

Richard D. Ryder

SOCIETAS

essays in political
& cultural criticism

imprint-academic.com

Published in the UK by Societas
Imprint Academic, PO Box 200, Exeter EX5 5YX, UK

Published in the USA by Societas
Imprint Academic, Philosophy Documentation Center
PO Box 7147, Charlottesville, VA 22906-7147, USA

ISBN 184540 047 X
9781845400477

A CIP catalogue record for this book is available from the
British Library and US Library of Congress

Contents

Introduction

The rules of the game are changing
Tony Blair, BBC Panorama, 9 October 2005

Contemporary Western politics often lacks two things: a moral theory and a respect for the facts. Power, party and pragmatism have become paramount and spin more important than substance. Remnants of respect for the ideals of democracy, human rights and liberalism remain but these are often vaguely defined and inconsistently applied. Is it possible to rediscover or redefine some clearer sense of moral purpose in politics? To increase its concern for truthfulness and to base it upon some transparent moral objectives? The moral vacuum in Western politics today all too easily could be filled by blind patriotism, religious fundamentalism, commercialism or naked power. This book is not merely a call for maintaining standards in public life. It suggests that morality and truth-seeking should be put back into the very foundations of politics. This is not a plea for a hidden agenda, for any sort of dogmatism or for any absolute idealism. It is simply a request that political policy should be based, not upon mere opinion, nor upon a set of knee jerk reflexes, but upon a scientific concern for the facts and an intelligent and open moral argument.

I suppose my own interest in political philosophy goes back to childhood. There were times when I felt so oppressed by those around me that I tried to work out how the situation ought to be put right. At boarding school I found myself in a police state in miniature. The supreme authorities were the teachers or, significantly, the 'masters', as they were then called. Their police force was the prefects who enforced a rigid set of rules with draconian corporal punishment. The regime was authoritarian and hierarchical, inculcating the militaristic virtues of mental and physical toughness and obedience to command. The traditional principles of liberty, equality and democracy were ignored. Indeed, inequality was enforced through a system of petty privileges; the sixth former could walk upon the lawn and have one hand in his pocket, the prefect could use an umbrella, the head boy could have a beard, a wife and two children — while the wretched new boy had no privileges at all! Only 'justice' was given some sort of respect — but this was a justice that was defined and administered entirely by those in power, and without appeal. We, the subjects of this totalitarian mini-state, participated in no political debate about the running of the school, nor were we permitted any votes in determining how policy should be administered. In daily Anglican chapel services we were subjected to selective Christian indoctrination; our virtues were to be fortitude, self-discipline and obedience to authority. There was no separate legislature, no independent judiciary, only an unyielding and unelected executive that controlled every moment of our lives. Such a situation caused great misery and fear for many of us. Some, however, prospered under these conditions; those who were exceptionally robust and those who toed the line. Others cracked mentally and disappeared. A few became rebels, some clandestinely and some more openly; this is one of the many paradoxes of the traditional British public school system — it has produced not only the great conformers but also some of the reformers of society. None of us were to be uninfluenced throughout our lives by these few traumatic years. Eventually, when I became a prefect in this little police state, I tried, rather ineffectually, to put some revolutionary ideas into practice. What, I asked myself, was the purpose of the school regime? A 'good education'? But what did that mean? As hard as I looked I could not see a clear moral vision on which school rules and policies were established, nor any body of hard factual evidence to support them.

This book proposes re-inserting moral principles into politics. I suggest these could be Utilitarian, Kantian, Aristotelian, Rights Theory, post-Christian or something new; the important point is that they should be argued clearly, open to dissent, and applied more or less consistently. Currently, it is impossible to debate political morality with most politicians because they do not have a coherent moral position. Instead, they utter an odd assortment of moral clichés and assumptions. While paying lip service to human rights, for example, they nevertheless tend to assume that the moral goodness of a policy depends upon the *total number of people* who benefit from it, often overlooking the interests of the individual. My own moral position (painism) attempts to reverse this trend, claiming that it is only the individual that matters (Ryder 2001), and holding that the suffering of individuals should be our chief moral concern. As we shall see, this challenges democracy's main weakness—its so-called 'tyranny by the majority'. I believe that underlying all the traditional aims of politics—the attainments of liberty, equality or justice (which are analysed in detail in part 1)—is the search for happiness. Indeed, I would say that happiness, however unpopular the word itself may have become, should, nevertheless, be the real aim of politics. The wellbeing of the individual still faces two great political threats: the threat of the democratic majority and the threat of the state itself, whether or not it is democratic. Both threats must be challenged if the happiness of the individual is to be secured.

If politics is about helping individuals to be happy then it needs to find out from psychology how to do this. This is just one instance where science should play a greater role in establishing the facts in politics. There is a common failure to base political policies upon scientifically established truths. Most of the claims of political philosophers, too, have been untested scientifically. We may breezily assert that justice leads to freedom or that equality leads to justice, and a host of other things, but these claims are rarely tested scientifically, although some now could be.

My own experience of politicians at national level is that most of them are exceptionally decent people, although under far more searching moral scrutiny than are most of us, and far more likely to face angry charges of moral inconsistency, hypocrisy and mendacity. Nevertheless, we live in an age that is suspicious of politics. Over the last twenty years an average of only 18% of the British public have believed that politicians generally tell the truth. Why is this? Is this the fault of the politicians themselves or the media? Surely it would help if we knew what the politicians are really trying to achieve. This would increase their credibility. But we listen to them in vain for a convincing, coherent and consistent philosophy underlying their day to day manoeuvres. What we do find is 'sleaze' and a growing bureaucracy—a 'nanny state' that, with the proliferation of street CCTV cameras, the proposed introduction of identity cards, telephone-tapping, the politicisation of the police and new antiterrorist legislation, increasingly resembles George Orwell's nightmare vision; worst of all, we see an increasing toleration of the practice of torture. There is a strange post-Marxist notion in the air that politics and morality should be disconnected. Even stranger is the idea that their disconnection is both necessary and, in some way, right. This book challenges all these assumptions. Idealism itself can become dangerous. But going too far in the other direction, towards relativism, amoral expediency and opportunism, is equally perilous.

When Niccolo Machiavelli published *Il Principe* in 1513 he contested the then accepted Christian virtues by urging that rulers could use both force and fraud to protect the stability of the state and the welfare of its citizens. He argued that such laudable ends justified immoral means in a world where corruption and violence already prevailed and where entirely virtuous tactics were bound to fail. In effect, Machiavelli tried to take morality out of politics. So powerful has been the influence of Machiavelli's advice that, to this day, politicians and political philosophers frequently seem to assume that politics, because of its impact upon the lives of so many, not only allows, but rightly requires, violations of normally accepted moral standards. Of course, when faced by a Hitler or a Stalin, polite tea-table agreements count for little, and force and deception may become necessary. But this does not mean that moral considerations should be avoided. Quite to the contrary, it is precisely because of the gravity and the far reaching effects of politics that morality becomes exquisitely important. The lives and happiness of millions are at stake. It has been argued that in politics temptations to lie, steal, betray or even kill are far more compelling than in private life. But even if this is true, it is surely not a justification for throwing overboard all the usual moral scruples. If politics is often more morally testing than ordinary life, then this merely underlines why the relationship between morality and politics should be a close one.

Over the centuries, despite Machiavelli, politicians in Europe continued to justify their policies upon religious grounds: both sides in a war, for example, would claim that God was on their side. Various secular philosophers then began to add their contributions: Hobbes, Locke, Rousseau, Paine, Bentham and Mill — all could be said to be suggesting new moral bases for politics. The twentieth century, however, so active in every other way, began with a crisis in ethics; while the professional ethicists withdrew from public debate and became absorbed in obscure academic arguments among themselves, the politicians, mumbling as they did so about 'honour', drifted into two world wars. In 1945 there was a moral rebirth with the creation of a welfare state in Britain, the establishment of liberal democracies and increased political cooperation and interdependency in Europe. Despite, or perhaps because of the silence of the ethicists, huge new moral steps were taken with the founding of the United Nations in 1945, and the revival of international interest in the concept of human rights, typified by the passage of the Universal Declaration of Human Rights in 1948. This followed the Nuremberg War Crimes Tribunal which had dramatically spotlighted the Nazi atrocities, creating new offences such as crimes against peace and the crime of waging aggressive war. The charge of crimes against humanity for the first time held soldiers and officials liable for offences against individual citizens, whether foreigners or nationals. Hitherto, a state's killing of its own citizens had not been an established international offence. Much of the initiative for these moral and legal developments came from the US State Department following the line of Franklin Roosevelt's 'Four Freedoms' speech of January 1942 in which he had given, as the moral basis for US participation in World War Two, the defence of the freedoms of speech and worship, and from want and fear. Despite subsequent periods of stagnation due to the Cold War, gradual progress was marked by the UN Commission on Human Rights and by new UN treaties against torture (1984) and to protect women (1979) and children (1989).

It can be seen that the injection of the idea of human rights into the mainstream of international politics has been a most important moral development. It forms a strong moral basis for action. Nevertheless, there is still a chasm between these foundations and the formulation and rationale for detailed policies, and particularly for domestic ones. Some fifty rights are listed by the United Nations yet these are rarely cited by political leaders as the reasons for their actions. Why? Is it that the concept of rights is not accepted or that the problems of the rights theory approach are considered to be too great? Is there a need for an alternative moral language?

Uncertainty over the basis of rights has also been unsettling. Are rights self-justifying? Concepts such as 'humanity', 'human nature' and 'human dignity' have proved unsatisfactory as foundations for rights (Dunne & Wheeler 1999). Indeed, some cultures challenge the acceptance of the very concept of rights itself. Yet even with its quite different communal and hierarchical tradition China, for example, has signed the Vienna Declaration on Human Rights of 1993. Nevertheless, difficulties with this future superpower's attitude to human rights will persist. Is the alleged absolutism of the rights approach, which often seems to deny the possibility of trading off some people's rights in return for the enhancement of others' rights, going to prove to be too great a problem for China to accept? Although rights in general are assumed to have an absolute quality, in fact the UN treats only one right as absolute – the right not to be tortured. Would a more graded approach, which does not regard rights as absolute trumps, be a more acceptable basis for global agreement? Perhaps the culture of China, now a nation of individualised 'only' children, will itself change so as to accept the individualism of the West in due course. (Only-children can be supremely narcissistic and wilful. I fear for a future dominated by a China where such figures are in charge.)

The human rights revolution of recent years has come under attack from several quarters: Islamicists have seen it as Western or Christian imperialism, conservatives have viewed it as a device for undermining the authority of the state, and others as a manifestation of an ever expanding nanny bureaucracy (Ignatieff 2001). There are even criticisms that the growth in human rights legislation is an attempt by unelected lawyers to take over from elected politicians! As we have seen, the growth in international law, based upon human rights, has been a feature since 1945. Since the Presidency of Ronald Reagan, however, the US has set itself against such constraints and has opposed the powers of the International Criminal Court established to try those charged with crimes against humanity. But without such effective judicial mechanisms to enforce human rights we will be in difficulties and, although no-one would deny that human rights has been and remains a magnificent moral concept in post world war politics, it may now be running out of steam.

The aims of the so-called 'Third Way' could also be described as a moral agenda (Giddens 1998, 2000). Closely allied with the philosophies of New Labour in Britain and of Bill Clinton in America, the Third Way was described as extolling 'equal opportunity, personal responsibility and the mobilizing of citizens and communities'. With rights, so it said, come responsibilities. In America, it promoted wealth creation, fiscal discipline, health care reform, investment in education and training, welfare-to-work schemes, urban renewal and being tough on crime. It sought a dynamic and free market economy – 'the state should not row but steer'. Its critics accused the Third Way (and New Labour) of being unacceptably authoritarian as regards crime and education, careless of human rights, neglectful of the environment and of failing to contest inequalities in wealth and power. The Third Way clearly tried to combine the benefits of the welfare state with those of a vibrant and free economy, making an electorally attractive package. But did it really answer the fundamental questions on the ultimate moral purpose of politics?

The Iraq war of 2003 has proved to be a turning point. In Britain, many voters were outraged by the war and over a million marched in protest. They felt that the British government had given them neither *the facts* (about weapons of mass destruction) nor the *moral justification* for going to war and killing and injuring thousands in their name. Most agreed that the removal of a cruel dictator was a good thing, but were rightly concerned about the tens of thousands of innocents killed and mutilated in the process. The war illustrated what is lacking in modern politics. First, without reliable intelligence, the war was allowed to proceed on the basis — 'in the absence of any firm evidence that there are fairies at the bottom of the garden (i.e. weapons of mass destruction), we shall assume that there are'. Secondly, no coherent moral purpose for the war was provided by Coalition governments. In the place of rational moral argument there were only a few naive and inconsistent assertions — the emotive ramblings of philosophical amateurs such as George Bush and Tony Blair (Singer 2004). Yet US electors chose 'moral values' as the most important issue in the Presidential election that followed. Incredibly, most voted for Bush.

In the twenty-first century politicians cannot continue, surely, to pass laws and wage wars without explaining clearly to their peoples the precise moral arguments behind their actions, and their factual basis. A sound moral argument requires both factual and moral premises. Yet there has been little intelligent dialogue at either level. The mumbling of slogans must no longer suffice. We must demand more of our leaders, a few of whom are clearly morally blind (the sign of the psychopath) while others seem incapable of moral consistency. If they are not professional ethicists themselves then they should be advised by professional ethicists; they might then, at least, produce lucid and rational arguments to justify the decisions they take. Perhaps the title of this book — *Putting Morality **Back** into Politics* begs the question: was morality *ever* in politics? I like to believe that sometimes it has been. Certainly it should be.

Part I of the book goes back to basics and sketches an overview of traditional and contemporary political philosophy as it relates to the moral foundation for public policy, while Part II considers some psychological issues, outlines the moral theory of painism and suggests a way of putting it into politics (Ryder 2001). Painism happens to be the moral argument that I am proposing but, frankly, any decent moral theory, openly argued, would be better than none!

PART I

What Does Political Philosophy Say About Morality?

We have not discussed enough our ethical foundations

Gordon Brown, Brighton, 26 September 2005

Politics is about power. It is about those who make the decisions, what these are and how they are enforced. In the rough and tumble of the political process, however, in the maelstrom of plots and personalities, spin doctors and speeches, there is rarely time to step back and coolly analyse what is going on. This is where political philosophy comes in. It addresses a number of the basic questions, among them — what is the aim of politics? What is the relationship between politics and morality? Where do justice, equality, liberty, community, human rights and democracy fit in? From where does the state derive its authority and why do we, as individuals, owe it any obligation? I will overview much of what has been said on these questions, and conclude that politics should be the gentle application of a publicly argued morality.

The Philosophers

According to *Plato* (circa 429–347 BC), democracy is mob rule and so political decisions should be left to the experts, to rulers who are specially trained as philosophers. Who, then, ensures that these philosopher-kings are not themselves mistaken or corrupt? Plato replied that, in order to avoid the possibility of corruption, these rulers should not be allowed any private wealth. Why, then, should anyone want the job? Who would have the power to stop them changing the rules to their own advantage? How would they be appointed and dismissed? How would such impecunious rulers prevent those with wealth (and thus military power) from taking over? Would their philosophical skills really be sufficient for the job? Does ruling not also require other qualities such as practicality and factual knowledge?

One of Plato's pupils was *Aristotle* (384–322 BC) who rejected Plato's idea of an ideal state. Good government, said Aristotle, was constitutional, while bad government was arbitrary. Aristotle became a tutor to several rulers, most notably to the young Alexander the Great. He may have taught them to be philosopher-kings but Aristotle did not completely agree with Plato's view that only experts should rule. He advocated middle-class involvement in politics and suggested that virtuous male citizens (but not slaves or women) should participate in law-making and magistracy.

After the Greeks and the Romans, European thought on the subject of political theory was subsumed almost entirely by religion. The aim of politics and its moral direction was, theoretically, to do the will of God. Rulers claimed, in varying degree, to be divinely approved and, therefore, to be acting on God's behalf. For centuries, the rights of kingship went almost unquestioned, although a perennial tension persisted between the powers of church and state and, after the Reformation, between religious factions. Thousands died in religious wars. With the Renaissance, a more detached view of politics reappeared in the writings of *Niccolo Machiavelli* (1469–1527) whose theory of statecraft departed from Christian morality in arguing that the protection of the state from internal or external danger, and the welfare of its citizens, justified the use of both fraud and force. These ends, Machiavelli said, justify a ruler's means. Implicitly, Machiavelli was promoting two moral objectives: the safety of the state and the welfare of citizens, but he was proposing that these could be achieved by immoral methods. He is remembered for urging politicians to be concerned with power rather than with virtue. *Thomas Hobbes* (1588–1679), writing during the terrors and turbulence of the English Civil War which culminated in the overthrow and execution of King Charles I, defended absolutist government as the best alternative to anarchy and disorder. In his classic, *Leviathan*, of 1651, he depicted human beings as being naturally motivated to advance their own interests in the continuous 'war of every man against every man'. The only way to avoid life becoming 'nasty, solitary, brutish and short' was to exchange personal freedom for personal safety by handing over authority to a sovereign individual or group. Hobbes argued that, in return for enforcing a safe society, the sovereign should be entitled to obedience from the many. The sovereign power may disregard individual liberty, Hobbes said, and can enforce any laws it chooses. In many ways Hobbes' political philosophy can be seen as the yearning for security of a man whose life had been led in fear. *John Locke* (1632–1704) was also affected by the Civil War but was a consistent opponent of absolutism. Indeed, as an architect of the 'Glorious Revolution' of 1688, which peacefully replaced one king with another, he played a part in establishing a constitutional monarchy. Repugnance with the war and its aftermath led Locke to advocate a degree of toleration and freedom of conscience. Each individual has rights to life, liberty and property, Locke claimed, and it is the proper function of political authority to protect these rights. If it fails to do so, the people have a right to resistance, and even to revolution, in order to replace an unjust government.

Revolution became a much discussed topic among politicians and philosophers after the French Revolution of 1789. *Edmund Burke* (1729–1797) staunchly opposed it, asserting the value of tradition, experience and history. Governments can, said Burke, prevent evil but can only rarely promote good. They should allow some social change, however, in order to conserve traditional values, established customs and inherited rights. *Jean-Jacques Rousseau* (1712–1778) would not have agreed. As a prophet of the French Revolution he attacked most eighteenth century forms of government on the grounds that they deprived the people of the liberty of governing themselves. Rousseau proposed a radical democracy based upon his ambiguous notion of the general will — or the will of 'all acting selflessly'. Another, but entirely different, revolutionary inspiration was that of the American *Thomas Jefferson* (1743–1826) who followed Locke in asserting that humans have God-given 'natural' rights. Whereas Locke emphasised the rights to 'life, liberty and property', Jefferson significantly altered this to 'life, liberty and the pursuit of happiness'. Jefferson, as the principal author of the Declaration of Independence (and the third President of the United States), opposed strong central government, stressed individual freedom and responsibility, and advocated increased public education and economic equality.

Immanuel Kant (1724–1804), impinged upon political philosophy in several ways. For Kant the 'rational will' is opposed to 'natural inclinations', and he was portrayed as justifying the well ordered and highly structured state, authority imposed from above, and ideals and government policies that are highly defined. Liberalism, relativism and anarchism can all appear as anathema to Kant's way of thinking, although Kant is a liberal in the sense that he sees each individual as capable of questioning and rejecting his own socially defined behaviour. Kant stands for calmness, deliberation, a rational concern for individuals and, above all, a sense of duty. As Jean Hampton put it (Hampton 1995):

> Kant believes we can determine political policies that are logically consistent, prudentially sound and properly respectful of each person as an 'end in himself'.

Kant proposed that a hypothetical social contract be used to determine which policies are just and morally acceptable. Few detailed moral rules emerge, however, and, if they do, they are cloaked in complication. By emphasising the *categorical imperative*, Kant's chief contributions to political philosophy have been the notion of *duty* and its role in reinforcing the ideas of a state's duties towards its citizens, of its citizens' duties to respect the law, of the probity of public office and of 'good governance' itself. Kant stands for the duty side of the rather facile duty–rights dispute that sometimes characterizes political conversation in the twenty-first century.

The interest in the idea of 'rights' was not entirely American in its origins. The rather underestimated Englishman *Thomas Paine* (1737–1809) was a supporter of both the American and French revolutions and in his *The Rights of Man* (1791), advocated democracy and a form of radical welfare state in order to abolish poverty and war. His scheme included old age pensions, child and marriage allowances and universal education. *Jeremy Bentham* (1748–1832) rejected the idea that rights were natural or God-given but, as a pioneer of Utilitarianism, advocated the moral theory that approves an action in so far as it promotes the greatest amount of happiness. To this end he supported widespread social, economic, legal and governmental reforms. Although Utilitarianism has had a formative effect upon liberalism it can also have illiberal consequences. The central flaw in Utilitarianism is that it can justify the oppression of individuals and minorities on the grounds that a majority benefits or, to put it more exactly, it can excuse any amount of suffering if it leads to a greater *total* happiness. This is the essential problem with democracy and is a difficulty largely created by the Utilitarian practice, when calculating what is a good policy, of *aggregating* the pains and pleasures of several or many individuals—a problem avoided by painism (see pp. 73–80). *John Stuart Mill* (1806–1873) applied Utilitarian ideas extensively to politics and, as a Member of Parliament, he supported female suffrage, workers' cooperatives and other social reforms. Mill is often seen as the most influential liberal philosopher of the nineteenth century, standing for the liberty of the individual against the arbitrary power of the state. Mill's Harm Principle is fundamental (Mill 1859):

> The only purpose for which power can be rightfully exercised over any member of a civilised community, against his will, is to prevent harm to others.

Mill was a staunch supporter of representative democracy but agonised over its principal problem which is that majority rule can sometimes oppress the interests of individuals and minorities. *Karl Marx* (1818–1883), the father of twentieth-century communism, was a contemporary of Mill and also lived in London. Yet they had remarkably little contact. Both writers sought social change and the liberation of the oppressed, but Mill was a reformer and Marx a revolutionary. Mill emphasised the liberty of the individual while Marx was more concerned with the inequalities of the classes and the authority of the state. The former employed sweet reason while the latter dogmatically asserted the so-called 'scientific' certainties of socialism. Marx argued that economic factors are the real determining force in human history. Capitalism, he claimed, is destined to be overthrown by a revolution of the working class that will culminate in a classless communist society.

In the first half of the twentieth century, against the background of two great world wars and the totalitarian regimes of Nazism, Fascism and Communism, the main contributions to political philosophy came from the German-speaking world. *Max Weber* (1864–1920) insisted on the distinction between facts and values. He championed a value-free and scientific study of politics and economics while respecting the subject's need for value. Weber condemned the rise of impersonal fact-based bureaucracies. *Hannah Arendt* (1906–1975) analysed the nature of modern mass society, attacked totalitarianism and advocated a form of republicanism. *Herbert Marcuse* (1898–1979) also condemned totalitarianism and, by promoting the 'non-repressive' society, was acclaimed by student radicals of the 1960s.

Friedrich Hayek (1899–1992) argued for extreme economic individualism. Any sort of state or other collective action threatens liberty, he said, and paves the way for totalitarianism. Hayek attacked previous claims that reason can create an ordered and civilised society. He believed that individual freedom is best preserved in a society that is allowed to evolve spontaneously. In order to prevent suffering the state should, however, provide a minimum income for the least fortunate. Hayek's hostility to socialist central planning, state ownership and economic equality appealed to the Reaganite and Thatcherite politics of the 1980s. *Sir Isaiah Berlin* (1909–2000) was actually born in Latvia but, like the others mentioned, he had seen the effects of totalitarianism, in his case those of Communism as well as Nazism. In the early 1960s he remarked upon the widespread belief in Britain that political philosophy was dead, and he sought to revive it. Berlin is now best remembered as a proponent of individual freedom, although his distinction between 'negative' freedom (from interference) and 'positive' freedom (to be one's own master) seems unclear in some cases — the same freedoms being capable of expression in either positive or negative terms. Berlin valued human beings as free agents and so attacked theories of historical inevitability. He rejected the idea that there are correct answers to all questions and so championed pluralism (a tolerance of different views). Berlin based this pluralism on his belief that we are faced with a range of incompatible ends that are 'equally ultimate', among these being liberty, justice, security, equality, harmony, peace and happiness.

Sir Karl Popper (1902–1994), surely the most important of these twentieth century philosophers from central Europe, also upheld liberalism and abhorred totalitarianism. For Popper, human knowledge is inherently fallible. Political theories, such as Marxism, fail to produce empirically falsifiable laws, nor do they, as Popper asserts is essential to a science, seek to test and falsify such laws. Nevertheless, he saw a similarity between science and politics: both are built upon traditions that are subject to critical review. Theories, like political institutions, *evolve* and the fittest survive. Popper championed the 'open' society characterised by reason, humanitarianism, freedom, democracy, egalitarianism and 'piecemeal social engineering', all ultimately aimed at the reduction of human suffering. He rejected wholesale utopianism as tending to lead to totalitarianism, and instead, favoured moderation and compromise. He warned against trying to explain social phenomena in terms of individual psychology (*psychologism*) or claiming to have discovered laws of history which can predict the future (*historicism*). The latter can lead, so he argued, to a form of amorality—the equation of moral goodness with so-called historical 'progress', even when this is attained through war or revolution. For Popper, capitalism should be subject to the humanitarian restraints of the welfare state. The chief advantage of democracy, according to Popper, is that it should provide a way for the people to dismiss bad governments. Along with *Jürgen Habermas*, who was born in 1929, and who also argued against the determinism of Marxism, it can be seen that all these writers share an antipathy towards the totalitarian state and all, in varying degree, proclaim the advantages of democracy and rational debate. This is the gist of their political morality.

The Anglo-American political philosophers of the twentieth century form a more diverse group with *Michael Oakeshott* (1901–1990) as the leading proponent of conservatism. Oakeshott, an Englishman, argued that social reality is beyond the capacity of human thought to comprehend and that, therefore, all ideology is worthless or even dangerous. Politics and morality should be kept apart. In place of ideology, Oakeshott urged a pragmatic approach grounded in tradition. He despised 'technical' (or 'cookery book') knowledge and preferred the 'practical' knowledge gained through experience and passed on through apprenticeship. He attacked political rationalists with their merely 'abstract' recipes, who make mistake after mistake, causing war and chaos. Although Oakeshott condemned a prescriptive approach to politics he nevertheless prescribed individual freedom and social stability. 'The enterprise is to keep afloat on an even keel,' he said. The correct role of government is to act as an umpire whose business is merely 'to administer the rules of the game'. He condemned the welfare state as a threat to individual freedom. Oakeshott extolled the authority of tradition while, paradoxically, appearing to reject the traditions of charity and rationalism that go back some two thousand years.

John Rawls (1921–2002) is the American political philosopher whose work has dominated the whole field of political philosophy since his *Theory of Justice* was published in 1971. In it he presents an alternative to Utilitarianism in the form of three liberal principles that should be applied in a just society. The first, the Liberty Principle, is that:

> each person is to have an equal right to the most extensive total system of equal basic liberties compatible with a similar system of liberty for all.

and the second and third principles are:

> social and economic inequalities are to be arranged so that they
> are both (a) to the greatest benefit of the least advantaged, and (b)
> attached to offices and positions open to all under conditions of
> fair equality of opportunity.

In the above, (a) is usually called the Difference Principle and (b) the
Fair Opportunity Principle (Rawls 1972).

The first principle (which safeguards basic liberties such as freedoms of speech, thought, conscience, assembly, movement, person
and property, as well as freedom from arbitrary arrest) takes priority
over the second and third, where (b) (equality of opportunity) takes
priority over (a) (the greatest benefit to the least advantaged). Overall, Rawls is proposing that societies should be arranged so that all
benefits should be 'distributed equally, unless an unequal distribution is to everyone's advantage.' Clearly, there are apparent contra-
dictions in such a position, and these have generated a huge
literature. This has been multiplied by Rawls' fanciful thought-
experiment for ensuring impartiality: he asks us to imagine an 'origi-
nal position' in which nobody knows what status (sex, occupation,
class etc.) they have. From behind this 'veil of ignorance' they would
choose, so Rawls argues, the society that he is proposing — one based
upon equality, liberty and the best conditions possible for the least
well-off. Many criticisms have been made of Rawls' approach arising partly, it seems, from the ambiguity of his theory and its complexity. The complexity derives partly from the theory's constant
shifting of emphasis from justice as the chief virtue of social systems
to other moral ends such as freedom, equality and various 'social
primary goods' (including 'powers, opportunities, income, wealth,
self-realisation, self-respect and personal enjoyment'). Rawls, however, accepts that there can be a plurality of such conceptions of what
is good and, provided they are reasonable, he tolerates them. The
state should leave people free to pursue their own enjoyments of
good things. He makes a distinction between what is *good* (and
enjoyed) and what is *right* (and morally obligatory).

Rawls's principles of justice define what is right and what the state
should impose through the redistribution of wealth, allowances,
sickness benefits, free schooling and so on. In his *Justice as Fairness : A
Restatement* (2001), Rawls sought to answer his critics and rectify the
faults he admitted in his earlier writings. He explains that his concept of 'justice as fairness' is not intended to be a comprehensive
moral doctrine but only a 'much narrower' political conception

although, as he admits, such political values nevertheless 'govern the basic framework of social life'. How, then, does a political conception relate to ethics? Rawls suggests no clear connection — 'most citizens come to affirm the public political conception without seeing any particular connection, one way or the other, between it and their other views'. Although Rawls avoids a proper analysis of his moral premises, words such as 'need', 'pleasure' and 'enjoyment' recur. Ultimately, he favours 'a reasonably harmonious and stable pluralist and democratic society' and one that is 'well ordered'. Why is it that philosophers so often express themselves unclearly? Is it because their ideas are genuinely difficult or are they themselves unclear as to what it is they are trying to say?

Robert Nozick (1938–2002), another American, was a leading exponent of libertarianism, proposing that governments have no business interfering with the natural rights of individuals, particularly the right to property. Nozick thus argues that governments should not tax individuals beyond the level required to protect them from war and crime. Any attempts by the state to redistribute wealth from the rich to the poor are ruled out. Taxation, says Nozick, is like slavery. If I pay 40% of my earnings in tax, without consent, it is equivalent to saying that 40% of my working week is spent in forced labour. Later, Nozick appeared to reject his earlier libertarian advocacy of 'the minimal state' in favour of a pluralistic democracy. He criticised Utilitarianism on the grounds that 'there is no justified sacrifice of some of us for others'; each individual is separate. In other words, Nozick implied not only that it is wrong to *aggregate* the sufferings and benefits of several individuals (as I claim in *painism*) but that it is also wrong even to *trade-off* the sufferings and benefits of one individual against those of another individual. What happens, then, when the rights of one individual conflict with the rights of another? According to Nozick the rights of an individual are absolutely inviolable. Does this then mean that the state must never coerce anyone? Nozick tried to refute this anarchistic claim by asserting that a minimal state is still required to establish guilt, determine punishment, pay compensation and protect the rights of all. He at least admitted, therefore, the implied moral importance of impartiality, justice and universality. Nozick's best-known contribution to political philosophy is, perhaps, his *Entitlement Theory*, in which he argued that the redistribution of goods cannot be justified by 'structured' principles, as proposed by Rawls, but only through a history of *just acquisition* and *just transfer* (such as selling, giving, loaning etc.) or when labour is 'mixed' with unheld resources. So two qualities, 'free choice' and 'labour', seem to emerge as the bases for the just transfer and acquisition of goods. Nozick's libertarian approach, however, leaves the wealthy under little obligation to help the poor. His *libertarian* ('right-wing') concern for rights has been paralleled by another American philosopher, *Ronald Dworkin* (b. 1931), whose promotion of individual rights has, in contrast, been part of a *liberal* ('left-wing') philosophy. Dworkin has proposed that rights be used as 'trumps' over cost/benefit calculations where inegalitarian factors are present. For Dworkin the interests of each individual matter equally.

In recent years, a proliferation of approaches has introduced new vocabularies being applied to the field of political philosophy from science, law and economics, and issues such as feminism, and the interrelations between ethnic and religious communities, have tended to take the centre of the stage. As Will Kymlicka has stated, 'justice' was the buzz-word of the 1970s, 'community' in the 1980s and 'citizenship' in the 1990s (Kymlicka 2002). What will be the buzz-words of the 2000s? A possible candidate might be 'political morality'.

Happiness

Why has there been so little recent discussion of our subject's ethical foundations? It has been as though each of the distinguished writers cited has tried to build his theory without examining its moral basis. Each has selected, apparently without much question, his favoured political principle of equality, liberty, justice, community, stability or democracy and flown with it, leaving clear air between his ideas and the ground. These are all moral objectives but they have usually been put forward without much explanation as to *why* they are considered to be good. It seems that much of the confusion and complexity in the field stems from this failure to examine ethical foundations.

In this section I will look at the link between political morality and happiness, seen by the Utilitarians as the chief object of politics. Morality helps us to decide the aims of politics — what the politicians should be striving for. Politics is, after all, a very powerful form of applied ethics and it is the business of political philosophy to discuss and establish the general ethical principles to be applied. Political philosophy can look at how society *should* be organised, reflecting, as Andrew Heywood puts it, 'a concern with what *should*, *ought* or *must* be brought about, rather than what *is*' (Heywood 2000). This creates a range of subsidiary moral questions such as 'who *should* rule?', 'how *should* wealth be distributed?', 'what *should* be the limits of individual freedom?', 'what *should* governments do?' and 'why *should* I obey the state?'. Moral values, concealed or otherwise, underlie every aspect of the political philosophical debate.

I happen to believe that all the great principles of political philosophy already cited are themselves subordinate to one overall moral objective which is the attainment of happiness, through gaining pleasures and reducing pains (i.e. suffering), and particularly the pains of the greatest sufferers:

- Why is *equality* deemed to be good?
  Because it can be a potent source of happiness.

- Why is *justice* deemed to be good?
  Because it can be a potent source of happiness.

- Why is *liberty* deemed to be good?
  Because it can be a potent source of happiness.

- Why is *community* deemed to be good?
  Because it can be a potent source of happiness.

- Why is *social stability* deemed to be good?
  Because it can be a potent source of happiness.

- Why is *democracy* deemed to be good?
  Because it can be a potent source of happiness.

- Why are *rights* deemed to be good?
  Because they can be a potent source of happiness.

These questions, all with the same answer, can be applied to a host of other political ends that are believed to be good; for example, peace, self-realisation, affluence and so on.

Perhaps there should be a field of political psychology which could more closely analyse the *degree* to which justice, liberty, equality and other political ends actually do have the effect of increasing happiness and, in each case, what the possible disadvantages are. Nothing is entirely straightforward in psychology. Years ago Erich Fromm, for example, suggested that some people are made insecure by too much freedom and feel happier when they find themselves part of some restraining structure. Many 'institutionalised' old lags in prison, together with some tenured university professors, would agree with this. Further scientific research needs to be done in such areas. To simply lay down moral laws enforcing freedom, equality, justice and so on makes no allowance, for example, for individual

differences. Nor does it take on board subtle changes in other circumstances. Conflicts between such principles also need to be
addressed: what, for example, should be the order of priority
between equality, freedom and justice? Which takes precedence? It
is only empirical psychological studies, surely, that can reveal their
relative powers as happiness-inducers.

Overall, however, all these traditional principles tend to increase
happiness. If this is the reason they are deemed to be 'good', why has
the discussion of happiness been so sparse over recent years, particularly among political philosophers? It was not always the case.
Aristotle and Plato discussed happiness at some length, and so did
Mill and Bentham. Somehow, the examination of happiness became
discredited. Anyone raising the issue today risks being regarded as
naive. Why is this? Two reasons occur to me. One is that the nineteenth century critics of Utilitarianism were successful with their
argument that happiness is difficult to define and impossible to measure. The second is that European culture over the last 150 years has
been militaristic in outlook, perceiving those who seem preoccupied
with happiness as being weak, self-indulgent and unmanly. The tyranny of the cult of machismo still runs deep in Western societies. The
traditionally more feminine concerns of care, compassion and contentment have not yet been fully established. There is still a military
ethos to the bodies politic of the English-speaking nations, and the
so-called 'war against terrorism' is worsening this. How can men be
made to fight if they are too concerned about their own and others'
happiness? Wars can be fought and justified so much more easily in
the name of freedom or justice, or even democracy! We have seen
this in the case of Afghanistan and Iraq in the twenty-first century.

Much of the confusion and complexity in the writings of twentieth-
century political philosophers originated in this failure to realise or
admit that happiness is the ultimate political objective. Writers try to
avoid the use of the term. Instead, as we have seen, they emphasise
the subordinate concepts of equality, freedom or justice. Yet, sooner
or later, the idea of happiness nearly always slips out. Despite their
use of turgid jargon, or alternative wordings, this is their underlying
message. Their arguments become tortuous because equality, freedom and justice sooner or later conflict one with another. Which
principle is to be considered the most important? Such arguments
are rather like quarrelling over the ingredients of a fruit cake. Is it to
be the fruit, the eggs or the flour? The answer, of course, is that if we
are trying to make a fruit cake then *all* those ingredients are neces-

sary. If we lose sight of our ultimate objective, a delicious fruit cake, we could find ourselves producing only an indigestible mess. Admittedly, there have been political writers whose ultimate aim has *not* been the happiness of society at large. *Friedrich Nietzsche* (1844–1900), for example, in arguing that the 'superior' type of human being rejects existing morality, expressed no condemnation of those superior beings who exercise despotic power over lesser people, presumably making them unhappy. Nietzsche's concerns were limited chiefly to benefits for the 'ubermensch', the superior people. Like Aristotle's, Nietzsche's main concern was with an elite of which he, himself, happened to be a member. Dictators over the ages have shown a similar disregard for the happiness of the masses, concentrating instead upon their own wellbeing and their pursuit of power.

In 1930 Bertrand Russell wrote a book about happiness that, in many ways, anticipated the development of the techniques of cognitive psychotherapy of fifty years later (Russell 1930). Russell points out that certain simple things are indispensable to happiness such as 'food and shelter, health, love, successful work and the respect of one's own herd'. For some, parenthood, too, is essential. In addition to these things, so Russell says, it is imperative that our 'passions and interests are directed outward, not inward'. We must avoid self-centred passions such as 'fear, envy, the sense of sin, self-pity and self-admiration — in all these our desires are centred upon ourselves: there is no genuine interest in the outer world'. The answer is to cultivate, through prolonged mental exercises, genuine outer-directed interests. Self-denial is not the answer, says Russell, because a person needs to be integrated with the world, 'untroubled by the thought of death because he feels himself not really separate from those who will come after ... it is in such profound instinctive union with the stream of life that greatest joy is to be found'. Today, we can certainly concur with Russell that happiness is associated with the satisfaction of wants and needs; these include not only basic needs for food, water, warmth, comfort, sexual satisfaction, sleep and health, but also more psychological requirements such as self-identity, self-esteem, security, affection, sense of family, intellectual and aesthetic stimulation and friendship. If any of these are not satisfied then suffering tends to follow. Psychologists, like political philosophers, have been inclined to avoid the term 'happiness', preferring to reduce behaviour and experience to smaller and more manageable components.

Michael Argyle, however, was an Oxford psychologist who studied the subject for many years and concluded that some of happiness's main causes are health, good relationships, job satisfaction, leisure interests and, to an extent, affluence (Argyle 1987). High expectations that cannot be met are found to be a common source of unhappiness, as various other scientists have confirmed (Nettle 2004). Paul Martin has stressed 'connectedness' (having closer relationships) as one of the most important and universal features found in happy people (Martin 2005). Engagement in meaningful activity, a sense of purpose, resilience, self-esteem, control of one's life, optimism, playfulness, an outward focus, humour, wisdom, challenges and freedom from excessive materialism are also common. But are these the causes or the effects of happiness? Or both? A happy person sees things through rose tinted spectacles. Much depends upon *mood* which is caused by the right balance of chemicals such as serotonin and dopamine in the brain. Genetic factors can play a part in mood. Losses generally cause depression, but depression can also 'just happen' for no apparent external reason when serotonin levels sag spontaneously. Wins or 'rewards' (caused by the satisfaction of drives or by drive-less pleasures) tend to cause joy, but less so with repetition.

American psychologists and economists have recently begun to use happiness as an indicator of a country's success. But they have fallen into the Utilitarian trap of measuring happiness as the *aggregation* of the happinesses of large groups of individuals. They have found that women report that having sex, relaxing with friends and having lunch with colleagues bring the most enjoyment, followed closely by watching television alone. The construction of a national 'wellbeing account' has been proposed. In general, psychologists now consider that happiness can be measured validly and reliably, that social policies can improve happiness and that happiness promotes altruism, sociability, activity, initiative and health (Veenhoven 2003).

We can also see how some of the classic ideals of political philosophy tend to promote happiness: liberty allows the individual to seek satisfactions for his wants and needs; justice avoids the feeling of being unfairly treated; equality boosts opportunities for self-esteem; democracy, too, tends to promote satisfactions for the majority and provides a sense of involvement. We can also see the list of human rights as an attempted recipe for human happiness, itemised in non-psychological language. Further research into the psychology of individual happiness should help politicians to know what they can do to increase it; an emphasis upon health and social services, full employment and the avoidance of war would, so it seems, make a good beginning. Politicians should use such science for the basis of their policies. Each political proposal should be accompanied not only by a certificate of moral justification but by a scientific audit of its effects upon happiness.

It has been suggested that the affluent and leisured upper classes have often been happy even though they have had little or no work to do. Uninfected by the Protestant Ethic of hard work they have felt no guilt about their idleness and no anxiety about their future material security. Nevertheless, they have tended to stick to routines and formalities and to have a belief in the superiority of their social status. The relationship between wealth and happiness is not straightforward but it seems likely that, although wealth does not guarantee happiness, poverty is likely to cause unhappiness. One survey has shown that whereas most people say they are happy 52% of the time, the rich say they are happy 77% of the time. Extraverts tend to be happier than introverts, while those who act out their painful feelings say they are unhappier. Such findings are quite complicated and suggest that much further research is needed. Overall, however, having children, being married and having good friends, relatives and neighbours, all tend to promote happiness (Veenhoven 2003).

There are obviously fundamental questions about happiness that still need to be addressed. How should happiness be distributed in society and how is it that its usual subordinate principles (such as liberty, equality, justice, rights and democracy) actually contribute to happiness? Liberty, equality, democracy and justice have been the moral building blocks of our subject for centuries. Let us look at the ways these great ideals may be morally relevant today.

Liberty

Individual freedom to do what one wants is one of the most elemental of urges. Each individual animal, human or nonhuman, manifests ongoing behaviours that are responses to external or internal stimuli. To prevent these behaviours by physical or other barriers causes a loss of liberty, and the ensuing frustration is a painful experience. Everyone feels frustration in their lives, either from moral restrictions, a lack of actual opportunities or through material or psychological factors. Anxiety and anger follow. Those who are severely frustrated can become passive and self-blaming or abnormally aggressive and wilful. The latter may try to identify a target for their anger, blaming (accurately or otherwise) the state or others for causing their frustrations. Some writers, such as Nietzsche (who felt extremely frustrated by the stifling Christian principles of his female relations), and some of the mid-twentieth-century German-speaking political philosophers (who had felt the frustrations of living in total-itarian societies), may devote much of their energies to formulating theories that are based upon this primitive urge for freedom.

It is clearly true that philosophies are partly built upon personal experiences and particularly on those of childhood. Experiences of exceptional levels of frustration are often found in the lives of liber-als and those opposed to the status quo. Liberty, typically, becomes their central theme. A subtle distinction can, however, be made between those who experience a compassionate form of restriction (as in Nietzsche's case), and those whose frustrations were imposed upon them despotically or cruelly. The former often tend to believe in their own special status or mission, while the latter identify with the oppressed generally. Among the former will be those *libertarian* philosophers who demand freedom for the individual to forward his often selfish power-seeking and material interests, while among the latter will be the true *liberals* who wish to see every individual free to express themselves and to realise their potentials. Thus are created the two, quite different, forms of political ideology that emphasise *freedom* above all other moral values — *liberalism* and *liber-tarianism*. Commentators have compared these two ideologies along various dimensions, most notably as regards their considered role for the state and the extent to which they propose that the state should intervene in the lives of individuals. Whereas liberalism stipulates that the state should protect the individual's rights to free-doms of choice, religion, movement, speech, welfare and so on, libertarianism advocates only a minimal 'night watchman' role for the state in that its only legitimate role is to protect the individual from physical danger. It is not only the 'size' of the state (i.e. its influ-ence over the individual) that varies in the two ideologies, it is also the content of the rights that are deemed should be protected by the state; not only *how much* freedom but *which* freedoms. Whereas mod-ern 'welfare' liberals advocate state protection of the individual's rights to education, health and social welfare, the libertarian emphasises the protection of the individual's rights to property and free enterprise. Whereas modern liberalism is seen as predomi-nantly 'left-wing', libertarianism is seen as a mainly 'right-wing' ideology that supports capitalism. So we can see that the concept of 'freedom' in political philosophy can mean many different things. After all, human drives are multifarious and people may want to be free to express any of them; not only to be free from poverty, illness and ignorance, but also free of any restraints on their acquisitive and other drives, bad as well as good.

For this reason I consider that one of the best ways of comparing liberalism and libertarianism is along the dimension of *altruism*. How far are we talking of our own *selfish* interests (our desire to be free of taxation, for example, as in Nozick), and how far are we concerned for the freedom of *others*? The locus of concern matters a great deal. In my opinion, morality is only concerned with others. Those who take a libertarian line are often preoccupied with their *own* financial and material interests or those of an elite with whom they identify, whereas those who take the liberal line include in their thinking the interests and rights of others generally.

How far, then, should a state restrict the freedoms of individuals? Surely, John Stuart Mill's solution to this, the central problem of liberalism, remains, in principle, the best—'the only purpose for which power can be rightfully exercised over any member of a civilised community, against his will, is to prevent harm to others' (*On Liberty*, see Mill 1859). Mill was particularly concerned to promote complete freedom of thought and discussion. Unpopular views need to be expressed, he said. If they are true, the benefits are obvious and, if not true, then they help us to reconsider and reaffirm our true views. Besides, beliefs are fallible and we benefit from constant openness to new ideas; only through free discussion can the truth be determined. We can never know in advance what benefits new ideas may bring. On the other hand, it has to be said that new ideas may also bring unhappiness, and Mill has no good answer to this problem. Knowledge gained from science, for example, is morally neutral, but it can be *applied* either for good or for ill. Mill reluctantly agreed that views that are almost certain to cause harm to others — the expression of racial hatred would be an example—should be suppressed. By 'harm', Mill means more than some trivial upset. If I wear a strange hat in the street I may upset my children and irritate a few other people. But this, surely, cannot be taken as a 'harm'. After all, somebody will take offence at almost anything. In the true Utilitarian tradition Mill was concerned about happiness, and for Mill, the main ingredients of a happy life are 'tranquility and excitement' (Mill 1863) Liberty is a means of achieving such a goal and happiness ('utility') is

'the ultimate appeal on all ethical questions' (Mill 1859). Giving people freedom of choice is more likely to make them happy, said Mill,
because they know better than anyone what makes them happy.
Furthermore, freedom allows people to develop their characters, to
test 'different experiments of living' and to achieve individual and
social 'progress'. Mill, however, claimed that intellectual pleasures
are superior to physical ones and this contention made it harder, perhaps, for Mill to make a distinction between real *harms* and trivial
upsets. If happiness can be treated as being a unitary variable (albeit
contributed to by a wide range of different pleasures — emotional,
sensual and cognitive) then one can say more easily that above a certain level of unhappiness *upsets* can be defined as *harms* and, accord-
ingly, be prohibited by law.

For Mill, then, state restrictions are allowed if they ward off genuine harm to others. Mere offence, however, is no harm. This raises
questions about such laws as those restricting prostitution and sib-
ling incest. Although they can cause offence, these practices need
cause no actual harm to others. Besides, and most importantly, they
are all voluntary. Is not free and informed *consent* a sufficient reason
for sweeping away any such constraints on liberty?

Such a question raises further queries as to the relationship
between 'consent' and happiness. Does consent signal an expecta-
tion of happiness? Usually, I consent to something because I believe
it will help me to avoid suffering or give me pleasure; in short, consent will probably promote happiness. It seems that consent is one of
a large family of linguistic shorthands for expected happiness;
among the others are 'wants', 'needs', 'desires', 'interests', 'agreements', 'benefits', 'choices', 'rights' and 'preferences'.

Karl Marx's main criticism of liberalism was on the grounds of
equality. In his opinion, in a liberal society each individual competes
against others, particularly as regards the acquisition of material
property. Some win at the expense of rivals. The communitarians,
too, have criticised liberalism as the cult of the individual. In the liberal society, they suggest, each individual becomes alienated from
others and the traditional values of society are abandoned. But why,
one may ask, do conditions such as 'equality' and 'traditional values'
matter morally? Only, it seems to me, if they are further stepping
stones to personal happiness. As I have already suggested, there is
no point in depriving the 'haves' of their property if it is not going to
be used to make others happy. If property is making the 'haves'
happy then it is doing a good job. The trick, surely, is to distribute

assets so as to reduce the sufferings of the greatest sufferers. Does this mean 'equality'?

Equality

I have suggested that political philosophers have tended to stand upon one or other of the traditional stepping-stones to happiness and have tried to make it the exclusive foundation of their theories. Just as libertarians and liberals have chosen the stepping-stone of liberty, so socialists and communists have selected equality as their basic aim. In the modern era the ideas of hierarchy and inequality, previously accepted as parts of the natural order, have been challenged almost universally. John Locke led the way by assuming that we are born equal and by arguing that nobody has a natural right to subordinate another.

Equality, of course, can mean so many different things. Many terms have been used: *moral equality* implying that each individual has equal moral value; *political equality* usually meaning that each person has equal political rights such as the right to vote, each person's vote counting equally; *equality of opportunity* indicating that each individual has an equal starting point and an equal chance to advance themselves; *legal equality* meaning equality before the law, in terms of rights and obligations; *material equality* (or equality of outcome) denoting an equal distribution of wealth, income and other material goods, while *social equality* refers usually to less tangible benefits such as prestige and respect. Each writer tends to refer to 'equality' in several of these senses. Moral, political and legal equalities are now widely accepted, at least in principle, in modern democratic societies (except in so far as foreigners and nonhumans are concerned) and so is the concept of equality of opportunity. Controversy centres more usually upon *material equality*, its desirability and achievability. If such equality is desirable, how far should it be enforced? To what extent should inherited wealth be permitted? Should attempts be made to constrain the unequal effects of 'innate' talent? How about inequalities between people in how hard they work? What about differences in acquired skills? How far should such inequalities be tolerated? What about the inequalities of chance and 'luck'? Should wealth reflect some combination of talent and hard work? These are some of the difficult questions that can be addressed.

The imposition of equality can, of course, infringe liberties, create injustice, fail to reward hard work and skill and so cause individual unhappiness. Enforced equality might also, surely, remove incentives and create both economic stagnation and a drab and colourless society. Is there, then, no justification for encouraging or promoting greater equality through the redistribution of property? As usual, we lack hard scientific data on the psychological effects of such redistribution. When 'freelance redistribution' occurs through fraud, theft or damage it can and does obviously cause pain. Similarly, the redistributive effects of normal business activity can also cause painful losses. Loss is the quintessential cause of reactive depression and depression is pure unhappiness. So we should be very careful about permitting the state, no less than a thief, to seize the property of one person in order to give it to others, if we are not to cause far greater suffering than happiness. Libertarians, such as Robert Nozick, oppose any interference by government in the property rights of citizens (except for the provision of protection against criminals and enemies) on the grounds that liberty outranks equality as a moral objective. Welfare liberals counter this argument by pointing out that Nozick's libertarianism would lead to greater inequalities in wealth, increased poverty and consequent loss of opportunities. On the other hand, writers such as John Rawls argue for the redistribution of property from the rich to the poor in deference to the claims of justice and liberty.

So, we see, again, conflicts between the principles of equality, liberty and justice. If these three principles are all stepping-stones to the more fundamental objective of happiness then the solution to such arguments surely, would be to measure and compare their effects upon the happiness of individuals. If we follow the principles of painism (see page 73), we should be looking, in particular, at the effects upon the levels of the suffering of maximum sufferers. Critics will no doubt reply that such measurements are impossible and that one cannot measure suffering. Well, if they believe that, then they are clearly out of touch with modern psychology. The behavioural effects of suffering, particularly preference and avoidance behaviours, are eminently measurable, and are now an established method of finding out the welfare of both human and nonhuman animals. With human beings one can also, of course, ascertain preference levels verbally. Admittedly, such technology is far from complete. When it is better advanced, however, answers will be found to such perennial questions as to which experience is the most important for happiness — justice, liberty or equality, and under what circumstances, and how, therefore, property should be distributed in order to reduce the pains of maximum sufferers. It has often been claimed that money does not lead to happiness. Whether or not this is the case, it is certainly true that poverty and financial insecurity both cause unhappiness. Does the perception of inequality also have a depressing effect? In the West, we live in societies of staggering material inequality. The richest people receive more income every hour than the average receive in a lifetime.

Nevertheless, in capitalist economies, profit provides an incentive, and free competition tends both to improve the quality of goods and drive down prices. In practice, modified forms of capitalism have worked well in securing a good quality of life for citizens. Yet, despite all its advantages capitalism still has its drawbacks, most obviously the tendency for the economy to see-saw from boom to bust, and a trade-cycle that induces much suffering caused by the loss of jobs and wealth. *Friedrich Engels* (1820–1895) claimed that, under capitalism, workers became involved in boring and repetitive tasks while their full potentials were frustrated. Such *alienation* was particularly characteristic of nineteenth-century industry; it was a significant source of suffering in Europe at that time, as it still is in some third-world economies today. It is also possible to argue that the focusing of attention on inequality is, through the creation of envy and resentment, another source of suffering. If I am poor but surrounded by poor people then my poverty hurts me less than it would if I was among millionaires; I feel less inferiority, shame and responsibility for my predicament. Handouts of money to the poor do not seem to be the answer. Yet a given sum of money causes much more pleasure for the poor than for the rich. A gift of £1,000 would cheer up most people but would probably be of total indifference to a billionaire. (This has been called 'the law of diminishing marginal returns'.) Indeed, one can argue that billionaires are so indifferent to a few thousand pounds that they would never miss such sums were they to be taken from them and redistributed to the poor. Such redistributions would almost certainly increase the *aggregated* total sum of happiness quite significantly and so would make considerable sense to Utilitarians. But do they make sense to a painist whose main concern is with reducing the pain of individuals who are maximum sufferers? Surely it would make sense to give joy to a handful of maximum sufferers by taking say, £10,000 from a billionaire who does not miss it.

Unconstrained free markets can produce appalling poverty and inequality. This is where great suffering is to be expected. But would not enforced equality, through the very high taxation of the very rich, suppress enterprise by removing incentives? Probably it would. Would other rewards — titles, medals and so on — prove to be satisfactory alternative incentives? Possibly, but only up to a point. One must conclude that some inequalities in society are probably inevitable and may, by providing incentives, make a more productive society than one that is forced to be entirely equal. A free market economy modified by a protective welfare state may be the best compromise. But is it just? And if it is unjust, does this matter?

Justice

Justice is the third historic moral good of political philosophy. It is another of our stepping-stones to happiness and it is the one particularly favoured by modern political philosophers. Sometimes 'just' has become synonymous with 'morally right' but, in its more particular sense, it has been associated with *fairness* and balance.

Aristotle described two forms of particular justice — distributive and rectificatory. *Distributive justice* allocates burdens and benefits fairly whereas *rectificatory justice* is concerned with maintaining a balance between two parties, either voluntarily or involuntarily (for example, through the imposition of penalties or rewards by a court of law). Justice can be concerned with the distribution not only of wealth but of any benefits including social status, liberties and rights. *Procedural justice* refers to the procedural rules adopted (e.g. rules of evidence and the use of juries) in order to achieve *substantive justice*, that is to say the outcome of such procedures (e.g. fines or other penalties). The phrase *social justice* is usually employed to refer to what is considered to be the morally correct way to distribute benefits generally, including wealth, property and income. Whereas libertarians and the so-called New Right dismiss such talk on the grounds that economic matters should be divorced from morality, liberals and socialists promote social justice as an important, or even as their principal, moral and political objective. For socialists the emphasis of social justice has been upon equality and community whereas liberals have emphasised individual freedom. The quarrel between liberals and socialists (who want a just society where everyone contributes to the best of their ability and where resources are distributed according to need) over their different understandings of what constitutes 'social justice' has thus centred upon the notion of equality, the liberals being prepared to tolerate some inequality on the grounds that this promotes liberty. Additional liberal arguments are that inequality (by permitting excellence) tends to equip society with wise and able rulers and supplies incentives for the economy.

Liberals have also argued that, provided there is *equality of opportunity*, it is morally right (or 'just') to give individuals their 'due'. They have, in other words, favoured a meritocratic society in which both talent and hard work are rewarded. This idea of 'just deserts' is, of course, difficult. To argue that someone is 'due' something because they are talented or decent or have worked hard, is problematic. How about those who, through no fault of their own, lack talents, cannot work hard because they are sick or handicapped or who, perhaps because of their upbringing, lack a conventional sense of decency? Or do all these sorts of consideration come under the rubric of equal opportunities? It seems suspiciously like a circular argument to say that social justice demands that 'just deserts' be recognised, as the idea of 'just deserts' already presupposes some agreed definition of 'justice'. We should, however, surely use rewards far more than we do, and punishments far less.

It would be wrong, I think, to omit from this discussion of justice some speculation on where the concerns with its two chief ingredients — fairness and balance — originate. I suspect that we are all innately 'hardwired' to be receptive to the notions of balance and fairness. Throughout history these ideas have been widely respected. I would suggest that balance and fairness are instinctively felt to be right and have often been applied to members of the moral in-group. Anthropological evidence indicates that a sense of fairness within the tribe has been practically universal. It probably has had survival value and so, almost certainly, runs far deeper than culture alone. I am not claiming that children will distribute their toys fairly among themselves without adult coaching, but only that the *idea* of fairness is present. A dominant child who seizes everything for himself still feels, instinctively, that something is wrong. Having more than one *needs* when others have less than they need, wrankles. In other words, humans have a *fairness instinct* towards their 'own kind', those seen to be the same as ourselves — relations, friends and fellow countrymen.

Gradually, this circle of perceived similarity has tended to expand, through improved knowledge and familiarity, to include all people, of all races and religions. Now we are expanding this moral circle to include individuals of other species also, based upon the similarity of sentience. (All who can suffer are considered to be within the moral pale; we are all part of the community of pain.) This *fairness instinct* is similar to, but not at all identical with, the more powerful *instinct of compassion* which I discuss elsewhere (see pp. 42–43, 56). Because they affect the way we treat immigrants, foreigners, those of different races and, indeed, species, these deep psychological mechanisms are still highly relevant to the formulation of a political morality today.

It is true to say that the concept of justice has played the dominant role in recent English-language writings in the field, led by those of John Rawls. His call for a basic framework of equal liberties for all (especially the equality of opportunity) and a concern for the least well-off, is based upon his desire to see a society that is just. Despite the oddness of Rawls' methodology, his conclusions look promising; he proposes, in effect, combining a market economy with a welfare state. But are his principles for regulating a society mutually compatible? Is it possible, for example, as Nozick has claimed, that Rawls' Liberty Principle conflicts with his Difference Principle? The former seems to require, among other things, the equal distribution of wealth, while the latter allows inequalities of wealth (provided that everyone, particularly the worst off, thereby benefit). Others have argued that a proper respect for liberty (the liberty to hold property, for example) would rule out Rawls' attempt to regulate property distribution through his Difference Principle. I see these muddles arising largely because Rawls is dealing with three different conditions that are deemed to be good — equality, liberty and justice — and not recognising that each are merely stepping stones to the fundamental good which is happiness. He is guilty of some muddled thinking. David Miller suggests keeping Rawls' demands for equal liberty and equality of opportunity but replacing his apparently self-contradictory Difference Principle (inequalities are to be arranged to the greatest benefit of the least advantaged) with a guaranteed minimum satisfaction of needs combined with a *principle of desert* (which tolerates inequalities in wealth, allowing rewards that are proportional to the individual's success in producing goods that others need and want) (Miller 2003). This seems to move away a little from giving preeminence to justice as our main moral objective.

Democracy

Democracy is the last of the four classical stepping stones to happiness that I will discuss in detail, and it is clearly less abstract than the others, being concerned with the *practical arrangement* of the state.

Nevertheless, it has become a clear moral good in recent American policy. Most writers, however, would seek to justify democracy in terms of other principles, claiming that it is a means to achieving justice, equality or freedom. So it is a second or third order principle — a means to others. For Abraham Lincoln, democracy was 'government of the people, by the people, and for the people' (Lincoln 1864). In antiquity, the Greeks saw democracy as being alternative to government by the aristocracy or the rich, although neither women, immigrants nor slaves were included in their democratic process. Other, typically modern, alternatives to democracy have included military dictatorships and totalitarian police states. Until the last hundred years or so democracy had a bad name, often being identified (following Plato) with mob rule; that is to say tyranny by an ill-educated majority. Since 1945, however, democracies have spread around the world working best, perhaps, where standards of education are highest.

There are two principal forms of democracy — *direct* democracy and *representative* democracy. In direct democracy the citizens themselves continuously participate in government through mass assemblies, as they did in Athens, or by other means such as frequent plebiscites. In representative democracy, on the other hand, the citizens periodically elect representatives to rule on their behalf. Forms of representative democracy, as recently developed and practised in the West, have served to enhance the reputation of democracy to such an extent that it is, early in the twenty-first century, almost universally accepted as desirable. The main features of such *liberal democracies* are (i) regular and fair elections (with almost universal adult suffrage), (ii) electoral choice (between candidates and parties), (iii) a market economy, (iv) constitutional rules, (v) checks and balances on power, (vi) an independent bureaucracy, (vii) guaranteed rights of the individual against the power of the state, and (viii) free and critical media. Of course there is much wrong with Western democracies, and none approach perfection. In the USA, for example, money counts for far too much in the electoral process, and in Britain, due to our 'first past the post' system, less than a quarter of the adult electorate can elect a government with a comfortable majority. In both systems patronage (the control of politicians' votes through the promise of lucrative jobs and honours) and the control of the representatives by party machines, distort legislative opinion. It seems desirable that elections should be proportional and funded entirely by the state, each party receiving electoral funds and seats proportional to the size of their popular vote.

Liberal democracies, perhaps unconsciously, produce a compromise between the Utilitarian mantra of majority decision and the Rights Theory concern with the rights of individuals. The advantages of democracies are usually considered to be that they can produce political stability, a sense of involvement and community, personal development, individual liberty and the respect for individual interests generally. In other words, it is claimed that life in a liberal democracy tends to be happier than in other types of regime. Against these claims, it is sometimes argued that under such democratic conditions demagogues and spin doctors prosper at the expense of truthful and wise rulers, and that, despite measures to protect human rights, the true interests of individuals and minorities can still be crushed by an ill-informed or selfish majority — the so-called 'tyranny by the 51%'. Democracies certainly tend to pander to short term popular opinion. The importance of free media, able to criticise and expose democracy's weaknesses, is clearly evident, but critics have remained: Marxists have continued to claim that liberal democracy is a sham which conceals the reality of control by international capitalist interests; direct democrats criticise representative democracy on the grounds that occasional elections are a poor substitute for direct and continuous public involvement in government; while some feminists have objected that most liberal democracies appear to be male-dominated and uninterested in extending democracy and equality into domestic and family life. Nevertheless, it seems that liberal democracy has succeeded where other systems of government have failed because it has gained popular acceptance, and it has achieved this popularity by creating economic *prosperity* and by its *responsiveness* to public opinion. This is the essence of democracy: that democratic governments rule, not in the interests of the rulers, but in the interests of the governed. Democracy itself is a great opinion poll; a mass preference test of what the majority believe will make them happier.

Today, there are additional ways in which the wishes of the electorate can be ascertained, other than via the media or through elections. Focus groups and opinion surveys have, increasingly, played a part in government. Although often derided they are, in fact, a legitimate way of discovering what people say that they actually want. They are a move away from representative democracy towards direct democracy. Traditionalists may complain that governments should lead public opinion rather than respond to it, but successful liberal democracies have demonstrated that, in order to remain in office, they must never become too much out of touch with public feeling. A government has access to many sources of information, especially from experts, to help it make good decisions. It can then, to an extent, inform and mould public opinion to its own way of thinking. The constant monitoring of the condition of the state, feedback on the effects of government policy, and information from scientific sources are all available to the modern government. Furthermore, if, as is often the case, a government knows the timing of the next election, it can gauge events so that the economic cycle and the beneficial effects of policies make an impression upon public awareness in time to influence voting. Such is the art of modern government in a liberal democracy.

Critics argue that democratic government has become too much a 'game of mirrors', of spin and public relations, when it should be about the difficult and hardheaded business of increasing efficiency and prosperity. Politicians are seen as talkers rather than do-ers; few, after all, have proved themselves to be efficient operators in the 'real' world outside of politics. The hopeful view is often expressed, however, that a government that is only able to spin images will eventually become unstuck at election time. Substance, so it is argued, still counts for more than spin in the longer term.

Clearly, the trend towards direct democracy could, with modern technology, be taken far further. Market research techniques can be harnessed to ascertain what people say that they really want and all electors could be equipped so as to be able to record their votes electronically, without leaving their homes, on a wide range of government decisions. How many would bother to vote on the more mundane issues, particularly if efficient governance meant that they were generally satisfied, is a matter for conjecture. And, if they were *forced* to vote, would this be an unacceptable infringement of liberty? Would it produce a valid expression of the electorate's wishes? Would it be real democracy? What is it that democratic governments should be seeking to satisfy? Some have argued that there is an important distinction to be made between people's desires and their real interests. Desires may be based upon insufficient information or may be merely short term, leading to pain or dissatisfaction in the longer run. The addict craving heroin is the epitome of this. Maybe a well informed democratic government should, like a good parent or psychotherapist, inform voters of all the possible consequences of their actions in advance, before they vote. The Prime Minister could become more of a chairman, sounding out public opinion, informing it and then implementing any decisions made.

Democracy matters, surely, because it is a means to majority happiness and this occurs not only because democracy tends to satisfy the desires of the majority, but also because people derive from the democratic process a pleasing sense of involvement. There are, in other words, two important sources of happiness contained in democracy — the happiness that occurs when desires are satisfied and, secondly, the contentment that people derive from being part of the decision process. Alois Stutzer and Bruno Frey have concluded that about two-thirds of the happiness deriving from democracy stems simply from this involvement in the political decision-making process (Stutzer 2000). Is this feeling of involvement so crucial, then, that we are prepared to reduce the efficiency of government to satisfy it? Is it going to make people happier if they can be involved in discussing an issue at length than if government makes the decision for them quickly? Maybe the inevitable delays caused by democracy sometimes mean that opportunities are lost or wrong decisions are made. Nevertheless, or so it seems, the feelings of unhappiness generated by being disenfranchised and unconsulted are sometimes greater than those caused by bad decisions.

The problems of democracy were apparent to J S Mill. He believed that direct democracy would be inefficient and so the only option is representative democracy. But how can the danger of electing dishonest flatterers and plausible orators be avoided? This is always a risk but one that is reduced by investigative and cynical media. Mill's main worry, of course, was the tyranny by the elected majority over minority opinions. He proposed that, through a system of proportional representation, minorities could at least be represented in Parliament, although they would still risk being outvoted there. The only way to protect them properly, Mill concluded, was to limit the powers of government so that it cannot interfere with certain areas of private life at all. There should be certain civil rights which cannot legitimately be over-ridden by governments.

Most of these problems are with us still. The failure of Western democracies to adopt effective forms of proportional representation lead to highly dubious electoral results, such as in the US Presidential Elections of 2001 and the British General Election of 2005. First-past-the-post electoral systems can lead to government by parties that are supported by far less than 50% of the electorate.

Money still plays an overriding and corrupting role in American and other democracies so that only those who are immensely rich stand any real chance of election. Millions of dollars are spent upon deceptive electoral advertising and biased television coverage. It seems that honest and truly proportional representative democracy that does not depend upon financial advantage, has not yet been tried. The US and UK are no longer the shining paragons of democracy that they sometimes imagine themselves to be. Understandably, under such circumstances, Third World critics suspect that Western attempts to 'export democracy' have become a code for exporting American culture and interests.

Nevertheless, Liberal democracy is the leading political system in the world today. Maybe its lack of clear morality is one of its strengths. It simply works. But since the arrogance of launching the Iraq war in 2003, the failure to enforce a fair solution in Palestine, the neglect of the hideous massacres in Rwanda and the failure to get to grips with global poverty, starvation and environmental crisis, we are entitled to question whether liberal democracy is enough. Liberal democracy creates consumer prosperity and a channel of communication between government and governed. It combines affluence and individual freedom. Yet it seems, at its worst, to be shortsighted, materialistic and neglectful of the interests of minorities and individuals. Jonathan Wolff asks whether democracy really deserves its high reputation (Wolff 1996). He points out that today's democracy can be criticised for its incoherence, its tyranny by the majority, its emphasis upon the election of *representatives* rather than on voting for *policies* on a day to day basis (direct democracy), its frequent lack of proportional representation and the populist 'mob rule' tabloid press tendency of which Plato warned us.

We can see that in liberal democracy a set of basic liberties takes priority over other values. Certain human rights (e.g. freedoms from arbitrary arrest and of speech, press, thought, religion, association, to vote and hold public office and private property) are guaranteed by law and, theoretically, enforced by the courts. These, to an extent, restrict the tendency towards the tyranny by majorities that is a feature of democratic systems. This tension between the power of the majority and the rights of the individual is an echo of the conflict between Utilitarianism and Rights Theory. The very idea that the wishes of a majority are more valid, or carry more weight, than the wishes of a minority is, itself, Utilitarian. So democracy can sometimes find itself producing mere convenience for many at the expense of causing severe pain to a few. Democracy is based upon the assumption that the wishes of the many always count for more than the wishes of the few, regardless of the *intensity* of those wishes. Democracy considers that *the sheer number of wishers is what matters*. To me this seems doubly at fault: at fault because it assumes that the *aggregation of wishes* is a valid procedure, and at fault also because it ignores the *intensity or strength* of wishes (and pains). This ambiguity goes back to Bentham and his famous slogan about 'the greatest happiness of the greatest number'. What did he actually mean? Was his emphasis upon the intensity of happiness or on the number of happy individuals, or on some ill-defined combination of the two? As we shall see, painism removes such ambiguity (see p. 73).

Vague awareness of the problem of 'tyranny by the majority' in liberal democracies has led to the development of a system of human rights and courts, some international, to enforce these rights. In other words, democracies have introduced a completely different moral system — Rights Theory — to curb the excesses of their basic Utilitarianism. So liberal democracies have become a strange moral hybrid: a Utilitarian/Rights cross. This works up to a point, but seems intellectually unsatisfactory. Rights act like stops on the slippery slopes of Utilitarianism. So, even if the overwhelming majority of a nation wants to destroy the handful of terrorists in their midst, the terrorists still have rights to a fair trial, for example. It is only laws protecting the welfare of *animals* that are still based almost entirely upon unfettered Utilitarianism whereas the laws protecting *human* welfare now tend to be tempered by the interests and rights of the individual.

One of the great strengths of Jeremy Bentham is that his Utilitarianism simplified and made workable what had previously been the hopeless tangle of English law (Ryan 1987). He provided a fixed standard by which the goodness of law could be estimated. Mill then began to complicate matters by introducing not only superior and inferior qualities of pleasure, but also such a concentration upon liberty as an end in itself, that many of his liberal followers began to forget that the ultimate objective is happiness and not liberty. This problem still afflicts liberalism today, and writers such as James Sterba have challenged the defenders of liberalism to give a 'non-question-begging defence of the particular conception of the good' that they endorse, one that is 'moral rather than self-interested' that includes positive as well as negative rights (Sterba 2002). Mill's teachings also began to swing the spotlight away from the *con-*

sequences of political action back on to the *character* of the moral agent, that is to say, back towards the acclaim of virtues. But with his passion for the eccentricities and qualities of the individual and for the freedom of minorities, it is not surprising that, for Mill, the main problem with democracy remained the constant threat of tyranny by the majority. This remains an unsolved issue, although it has been mitigated, as we have seen, by the late twentieth-century respect for individual rights.

Modern Issues

We have reviewed the four classical principles of liberty, justice, equality and democracy and their underlying and often unstated objective of happiness. Next, I shall briefly review some important contemporary issues, reflecting upon their relevance to an overall political morality. Among them are: *feminism, the media, welfare, religion, sociobiology, game theory, globalism and devolution, community, citizenship/immigration, environmentalism, human and animal rights, terrorism and good governance.*

Feminism

Nineteenth-century feminism concentrated upon female suffrage and, when this had been achieved, there was a lull before feminism erupted with renewed vigour in the 1960s. This second wave of feminism extended its concerns to cover all aspects of the domestic, social and sexual roles of women. Societies were attacked for their almost universal patriarchy and for the consequent exploitation and subjugation of women. Feminism insisted upon liberty, equality and justice for women in all areas of their lives, and the stereotypes of 'masculine' and 'feminine' roles were questioned. Today, feminism falls into three main traditions — *radical feminism* which sees gender differentiation as the most politically fundamental of all social divisions, *socialist feminism* which portrays sexism as a form of capitalist exploitation and *liberal feminism* which emphasises women's individualism and their equal opportunities and rights with men. By spotlighting a situation previously almost entirely ignored by conventional politics (with the exception of the actions of a few outstanding figures such as J S Mill himself) the feminist movement had, by the end of the twentieth century, achieved massive changes within the Western democracies and elsewhere. Feminism has sometimes emphasised the value of a more caring society and criticised the 'coldly' rational, abstract and aggressive approaches to

political issues allegedly characterised by male-dominated governments. Feminism has usually proceeded from the particular to the
general, valuing and using real experiences of gender-bias in pursuit
of its ultimate aim of ending men's systematic domination of women
(Mansbridge & Okin 1993). Feminism has, undoubtedly, given a
moral aim to politics. By attacking prejudice and discrimination it
has promoted liberty in the cause of justice and equality. This
enlightenment subsequently spread to other disadvantaged sec-
tions of the community and greater concern has been shown for
ethnic groups, the handicapped, children and sentient beings of
other species. The moral message is this: reject all forms of prejudice
and discrimination that are based upon moral irrelevancies such as
gender.

Freedom of the Media

In a democracy, the free media do an important job in exposing corruption and the abuses of power. Furthermore, the media have had
an important role to play in the two-way communication of ideas
and desires between governments and peoples. By questioning politicians they have sometimes forced them, however inadequately, to
attempt to justify their actions in moral terms. Indeed, the freedom
of the press is a very fine principle. But when that principle is
abused — as it has been by the British media — then it must be questioned. The so-called tabloid press in Britain has invaded the privacy
of individuals causing them intense distress, trivialising, over sim-
plifying, sensationalising, personalising and pandering to prejudice. It has cultivated hysteria and bigotry. More than this, foreign
owners of some British newspapers have successfully warped the
nation's political outlook on some issues in order to suit their own
international commercial interests. British ministers have been
brought down by the machinations of a handful of foreign and
sometimes corrupt millionaires. Yet the British public — in as much
as they have seen through this deception at all — have meekly continued to swallow the distortions, lies and moral illiteracy that the
nation's popular press has pedalled.

   The British media have also reinforced the stereotype that politicians are invariably corrupt and mendacious, and this cynicism has
tarnished the reputation of politics to such an extent that men and
women of genuine integrity and talent may be discouraged from
seeking political careers. The time has surely come to put things
right. Just as professional, charitable and, indeed, government agen-

cies are already held to account for the accuracy and fairness of their pronouncements, so also should be the press. The electronic media have long been constrained in such ways. Newspapers should *not* be permitted deceitfully to deceive their readers nor to foist their political objectives upon an unsuspecting public. They should be required by law to support their views, the substance of their reports and their selection of news, with facts, reasoned argument and moral theory. Reporting should be balanced, rational and accurate. Newspapers, no less than the BBC, should be required to be politically unbiased and balanced over a (defined) period of time. An elected press disciplinary body, independent of both government and the media, and subject to the courts, should be given far-reaching powers in law to penalise newspapers, radio and television stations and to fine and imprison editors and proprietors found wanting in these respects. Although the electronic media in Britain (but not America) has been far more accurate than the press in their reporting of news, a reluctance to allow governments to put their position has become established. Government spokespeople are constantly interrupted by interviewers and presenters who are often unfairly and automatically cynical or even rude. This merely makes it harder for governments to present properly reasoned arguments. In order to solve this problem there should be a rule that spokespeople can initially speak, uninterrupted, for an agreed period of time. Governments must be allowed, in a democracy, to put their case.

Religion

One reason why morality and politics have been kept apart is historical. Throughout mediaeval Europe religion played a powerful role in politics and was itself the cause of wars, persecution and oppression. In other parts of the world today religion still determines political decisions and, in the absence of a secular faith such as Marxism, often provides a source of aspiration for the materially deprived. Islamic extremism, as an expression of resentment against the sexual freedom, opulence and success of Western democracies, and, as an understandable protest against the support given by America to elitist Arab regimes and to oppressive Israeli administrations, has become an international problem. Does all such evidence suggest that morality and politics should be kept apart? No, it does not. It indicates that *religion* and politics should be kept apart. It is the blind irrationality of religions, their ignorance of science, their prejudice and fervour that are politically dangerous. Such qualities should, indeed, be kept private. There are, however, many good aspects of religions — their tolerance and compassion, for example that can play a role more publicly. Ethics can be quite separate from religion and should always play a role in politics. Indeed, secular ethics should play a far greater role politically. Of course, no single ethical system yet devised is entirely consistent or satisfactory so absolute certainty in ethics is impossible and dogmatism should be avoided. In Britain, there is a need not only to separate ethics from religion and its obsession with issues of minor moral importance such as sexual conduct, but also to encourage the discussion of secular ethics. Strangely, the BBC's ethical output is still almost entirely uttered by celebrities and religious journalists while expert moral and political philosophers are, relatively speaking, ignored.

Welfare

As a term, 'welfare' has sometimes crept into the political debate as a respectable alternative to 'happiness'. It works well as a euphemism, appearing to have a clarity and even the scientific credibility that 'happiness' is considered to lack. The emphasis of 'welfare', however, has been upon the physical rather than the mental. More specifically, the welfare state is one that takes responsibility for the provision of health, housing and social security. Educational services often are considered separately. Modern Western democracies follow one of three patterns of welfare state, either the *Beveridge type* which provides universal benefits based upon national insurance and taxation, the *corporate welfare state type* linked closely with jobs, or the *limited welfare state type* which provides little more than a 'safety net' for the extremely needy. The term 'welfarism' has been used by economists to express the view that the overall good of society is based upon the welfare of individuals, and that welfare can be measured by preferences.

Welfare theories sometimes appear difficult but they are, at least, recognising that welfare (or happiness) is the ultimate good. Far more could be done, however, to take into account the findings of science. As we have seen, happiness is a subject that is increasingly being researched by psychology (see pp. 20–22). In calculating welfare there is a tendency to overemphasise the moral importance of certain areas of the human condition such as cloning, gender roles, designer babies, parents' rights to choose the gender of their babies and so on. But far more important for welfare, surely, are issues such as bullying in schools and work places, the high handed treatment of

motorists by the state (as if people lose their human rights as soon as
they take the wheel of a motor vehicle), speciesism, world poverty,
global warming, international bad governance, voluntary euthanasia,
and the horrifyingly widespread use of torture in the world today.

Sociobiology

Sociobiology, a term coined by Edward O Wilson in his *Sociobiology :
The New Synthesis* in 1975, describes an approach to human behaviour based upon the idea that all or most social behaviour has a
genetic basis and has been selected naturally according to the principles of evolution. Behaviours such as dominance and male promis-
cuity have been considered as examples and, more importantly for
ethics, so have the propensities for empathy and altruism.

   Sociobiology can be seen as a reworking of the nineteenth-century
concept of *instinct* and its application to human beings as well as to
other animals. Desmond Morris and others had already revived this
tradition in the 1960s. It is a tradition that sometimes raises various
errors in thinking that were also associated with 'instinct', for example, that genetically determined behaviours of this sort are necessarily unconscious, inflexible, rigidly determined or uninfluenced by
environment. Sociobiological concepts, if carelessly applied, can
also produce some vintage examples of the so-called naturalistic
fallacy: that genetically determined behaviours are morally right, or,
at least that they are morally better than those that are entirely or
largely culturally or environmentally determined.

   Is there, then, any worthwhile connection between sociobiology
and political morality? By underlining that some of the differences
between human individuals, sexes and races are due to genetic
factors, sociobiology may discourage a naive approach to egalitarianism. But far more importantly and, as I have been arguing for
many years (Ryder 2000), altruism itself can be said to have instinc-
tual or genetic roots. This, if true, is tremendously encouraging. It
knocks on the head the perennial and pessimistic claim that human
nature is intrinsically 'evil' or invariably selfish. Our genes may be
metaphorically selfish, as Richard Dawkins has claimed, in that they
make us behave in ways that tend to multiply themselves, but some
of those genes, so I believe, also happen to encourage us to feel compassion for other individuals and to grasp very easily the basic idea
of fairness. Such 'wired-in' propensities to feel compassion and to
act fairly have helped our genes to survive. In other words, some of
our selfish genes encourage us to behave unselfishly! We clearly

evolved as social animals and the social cooperation that such *unself-ish instincts* have promoted has had a high survival value for our genes. We also have aggressive and acquisitive propensities within us that are plainly *selfish*, and the resulting conflicts between selfish and unselfish tendencies constitute the drama of life. We need moral codes that promote and culturally entrench the predominance of our unselfish instincts for fairness and compassion.

Game Theory

It is sometimes said that the famous so-called Prisoner's Dilemma (a classic thought experiment in game theory) illustrates how acting rationally but selfishly, without cooperating with others, does not always lead to the best outcome for anyone. The experiment imagines two guilty prisoners who are told that three conditions apply:

1. If both confess they each get two years in prison

2. If neither confesses, they each get one year

3. If only one confesses he goes free but the other gets ten years

The point to emphasise is that the prisoners are held separately and cannot communicate one with the other. So no cooperation is possible. Which, then, is the best course of action purely in terms of selfish physical outcome, regardless of ethics? Reason suggests that each should confess and get either two years or freedom with equal probability. (Not to confess means an equal chance of getting one year or ten years.) So, provided that both consider that imprisonment is a worse outcome than freedom, it seems rational for each prisoner to confess. This will land both in prison for two years. Yet if they had been able to cooperate by agreeing a joint strategy, neither would have needed to confess and so both would have been imprisoned for only one year.

It is claimed that many political situations are of this sort and can be modelled as prisoners' dilemmas or as a sequence of such situations. Yet the model seems to be highly contrived, the 'rules' governing outcomes being arbitrary. Furthermore, the outcomes are certain, whereas in real life outcomes are usually uncertain. In real life situations, as Steven Pinker reminds us (Pinker 1997), memory and emotion also play important roles; memories of the previous trustworthiness or treachery of a police chief, for instance, and feelings such as compassion, revenge or remorse will also influence decisions. Besides, political disputes and choices are often quite unlike the prisoner's dilemma in other ways.

Robert Axelrod (Axelrod 1984) has empirically tested an allegedly efficient 'tit-for-tat' strategy for real-life prisoner's dilemma situations, as proposed by Anatol Rapoport. This strategy dictates that we should cooperate with opponents until they fail to cooperate. If they fail to cooperate, we should do likewise by making an uncooperative move, and so on. That is to say, whenever they cooperate, we cooperate, and whenever they fail to cooperate, so do we. Once established, *tit for tat*, or *conditional cooperativeness*, seems to be an enduring feature in many human cultures. 'Do as you would be done by' and 'you scratch my back and I'll scratch yours' are examples of appropriate maxims. As Robert Wright has pointed out (Wright 1994), the feelings we have that encourage cooperation are friendship and trust, whereas those associated with lack of cooperation are enmity and mistrust.

So, in prolonged prisoner's dilemma type situations the computed results suggest that the tit for tat approach actually brings more benefits to all than do more obviously selfish strategies. Cooperation (provided others cooperate) actually seems to pay off. This does suggest that, under certain circumstances, altruism is, after all, in one's own selfish interest. For those with a cynical view of human nature this is a highly encouraging finding. It is even more encouraging if it can be applied to the behaviour of states and demonstrated that tit for tat fairness and cooperation, rather than war, are in the interests of all states. It is an argument for peace.

One obvious flaw to this approach appears to be that uncooperativeness, once established, may become permanent. If my opponents are also following the rules of tit for tat then it seems that the situation may become stuck with either permanent cooperation or permanent lack of cooperation. One failure to cooperate by either is disastrous. Is this the situation, for example, that obtained between the Israelis and Palestinians for so many years? An eye for an eye and a tooth for a tooth, continuously?

Globalism and Devolution

Globalism refers not only to the increasing economic and trading ties between states but to the growing credibility of international law, respect for the United Nations and the changed scale of thinking about the world. Images of our predominantly blue planet from space have helped the peoples of the world to see the world as a whole. The deeply wired human tendency to want to think in terms of ingroups and outgroups, of us and them, is now readjusting its scale. Vastly improved global communications and travel have also aided this change in perspective. We calculate our territorial attitudes and our concept of 'us and them', or *foreignness*, not so much on how far one country is from another *geographically* but on our degree of ignorance of the other country, its cultural differences from us and the *time* it takes to travel there. These are all being rapidly reduced. Television and air travel mean that more and more people begin to feel that those from other countries are not alien from themselves. The moral ingroup, once defined by the family or the tribe now, for many people, includes the whole human species and, indeed, other conscious species as well. But further psychological changes are occurring. Globalism, while reducing the feeling of foreignness, also produces feelings of insecurity. While accepting morally and intellectually that those from other nations are really very similar to ourselves, we also feel confused by the increasing scale, pace and complexity of globalism and yearn for more cosy and comforting feelings of home and hearth. We feel we are losing that pleasant glow of identity, of belonging, of being proud of being a member of an identifiable group. We need to belong to something familiar that *distinguishes* us from others. So we see wider economic and military alliances and greater moral and intellectual inclusiveness on one hand, while, on the other, we observe the promotion of smaller semi-autonomous political and cultural units. As Britain, for example, felt itself drawn increasingly into active roles in the European Union and NATO so, at the end of the twentieth century, it naturally disintegrated (quite peacefully) into the smaller, and partly self-governing, countries of Wales, England and Scotland. The old tribal feelings are now deployed in support of local football teams and the revival of interest in local customs and history. Ethically and economically we think big, while in terms of personal identity we like to think small.

At the start of the new millennium it thus appears that we are moving in two opposite directions. On one hand we see the growing influence of multinational corporations and global institutions such as the World Bank and the World Trade Organisation. On the other, smaller and smaller psychological communities appear, based upon old traditional senses of identity. Is this the beginning of the end of the nation-state? It certainly could be, although members of national governments can be guaranteed not to accelerate their own demise.

The creation of the big global institutions seems to be, in the context of changing technology, what is increasingly appropriate *economically*, while the devolution of powers to ancient and more culturally homogenous communities provides *psychological* satisfactions. In a small group we can feel valued: we can be big fish in a little pond. In the middle, recent and artificially established large nation states may get squeezed out. Such changes are not without risk, of course. Disputes over the boundaries of new and smaller communities can lead to wars, as among the constituent states of the old Yugoslavia in the 1990s, or wars between such communities and their old imperial masters who are reluctant to grant them autonomy (as in the case of Chechenya), and sometimes to a resentment and envy of the whole new order (as felt towards the West in many Islamic countries). In recent decades there has been a spate of independence and self-determination movements as the grip of the old militaristic empires has slackened. In many instances this has led some states to full secession. Some writers have claimed that political and cultural boundaries should coincide, denying the increasingly multi-cultural reality of many modern states. On occasions, consequent attempts to 'ethnically cleanse' territorial units has, of course, ended in tragedy and horror. When the United Nations and NATO have had to restore order they have, unimaginatively, tried to put the clock back by resisting the inevitable tendency of warring ethnic groups to want to separate. Such international interventions should take place promptly *before* ethnic atrocities occur. Once the atrocities have begun it is too late to patch up the differences and to expect two ethnic groups, bloodied by rape and murder, to live together again peacefully. Far better, then, to allow partition, and to ensure that it is done peacefully and equitably.

The twenty-first century seems, on the one hand increasingly global and, on the other, more concerned with the individual. Maybe large federations will prove to be the necessary link between these two extreme orders of scale. The move towards European federation was motivated more by the need to form an economic and political bloc large enough to stand up to the United States and by the desire to avoid European wars, than to a fear of the Soviet bloc during the Cold War. This move towards federation seems to be slowing. Of course, the national politicians of some EU member states, such as those in the United Kingdom, do not want to lose their political powers and many of the European media moguls are opposed to

European federation, some due to their personal and business connections with the United States. These reasons lack moral adequacy.

Maybe the spirits of compromise and moderation that are typical of some European cultures — especially since Europe experienced the horrors of two world wars — are essential if federations are to work. In other cultures, as in Iraq, for example, federalism has found it hard to take root.

Today, we live in a world of constantly shifting alliances — of massive trading blocs such as the EU, inadequately controlled by the World Trade Organisation, an expanding NATO, and by a United Nations that badly needs reform. What, then, of *world federation*? Does this await the togetherness engendered by invasion by an alien enemy from outer space or are human beings able to cooperate for less desperate reasons? Part of the moral significance of federation derives from the feelings of cooperation, security and community that it engenders.

Community

Broadly speaking, communitarianism has been a late twentieth century reaction against the rapidly changing scale and pace of the modern world, the anomie and feelings of insecurity that this has created and the perceived amorality and selfishness of some forms of extreme liberal individualism. As such, it was an understandable and, indeed, desirable reaction. A concern for *others* is, surely, the essence of morality. Communitarianism is sometimes defined as a political theory that puts an emphasis upon cultural and national values as being of greater importance than individual rights, and a belief that the individual is defined only or chiefly in terms of the community. Such a view can be found across the whole conventional political spectrum. On the right it manifests as a respect for the authority of the state and its traditions, in the centre as an attack upon laissez-faire capitalism, and on the left as a commitment to social equality or communism. The common thread is the subordination of the individual to the requirements of the group or community.

Too often, communitarians talk of the community as if it is a conscious entity, when clearly it is not. It is also unsettling that they frequently assume that the 'bigger' is of greater moral value than the 'smaller' — that the big group is thus more important than the smaller group and both are more important than the individual. This thinking is linked to the principal problem of democracy, majoritarianism ('tyranny by the 51%') and also, as I see it, to the main flaw in Utilitarianism as a moral theory, that is to say its aggregation principle (see pp. 74–76).

Morality is about what we do for others. It is not about what we want for ourselves. What I want for myself is a matter for psychology but what I *should* do for others is a question of ethics (Ryder, *Painism* 2001). But where communitarians make a mistake is in believing that individualism and selfishness are the same thing. They certainly are not the same.

Communitarians (whose hearts are clearly in the right place in their hatred of selfishness) also show another form of confused thinking. In hating selfishness they not only make the mistake of rejecting altruistic as well as selfish forms of individualism, but they also, quite frequently, reject entirely the notion of 'rights' in favour of 'duties'. The mistake here is to suppose that these two notions are mutually incompatible. They are not. In respecting the rights of another I am observing my duties towards them. Rights and duties are merely opposite sides of the same coin. To talk rationally and coolly of duties is perfectly acceptable but to become exclusively concerned with duties and responsibilities, as some communitarian politicians have done, smacks rather of the self-righteousness of the powerful being indulged at the expense of the sufferings of the weak: an emphasis upon the agent rather than the sufferer.

Will Kymlicka (Kymlicka 2002) has argued that modern communitarianism is descended from the third principle of the trinity of the French Revolution—'liberté, egalité et fraternité' which, for many years had been forced into subordination by the emphasis placed upon liberty and equality. Fraternity, or sense of community, has only resurfaced as an issue in political philosophy since the 1980s. Unlike the liberal view, where each individual is free to decide what is good, some communitarians argue that the state itself should define the good and then defend it. This seems to overlook the pluralism of modern societies. Imposing a 'common good' from above is unlikely to empower or satisfy oppressed minorities nor, indeed, the preferences of many individuals. As Kymlicka points out, modern communitarians often reveal a deep sense of separation anxiety. They write with foreboding about declining communities and lost values (Kymlicka 1993). They feel a nostalgia for 'the good old days' and lament the modern multicultural and permissive society. They yearn for some new 'team spirit' to hold us all together. It is clear that communitarians are the sort of people who are made to feel insecure by fragmentation, diversity and rapid change. They dislike adventures. Their contentment derives from dependency upon others and a sameness and predictability in their lives. They are home-loving folk. In the twenty-first century this is understandable as a reaction to rapid cultural change.

In conclusion, we can see that the communitarians' belief in the value of community is a reminder that many of the individual's sources of happiness are from relationships with others (see pp. 20–22) and from a sense of belonging to groups of various kinds. It is, however, wrong to argue that such sources of happiness are the only ones that matter or that they are psychologically or morally more significant than other sources of happiness. Although their cognitive content is distinct, such sources of happiness are not necessarily greater than others emanating from the good old principles of liberty, equality or justice. At its worst communitarianism can become nationalistic or elitist and, by undervaluing the individual, it can become separated from the basis of morality — which is a concern for the happiness of other *individuals*.

Citizenship and Immigration

As the peoples of the world move ever more freely around its surface problems inevitably arise. Thousands living in the poorer and more politically insecure parts of the globe understandably seek to live in the more affluent and stable parts. The USA, Europe, Australia and Canada, for example, have thus become attractive for political refugees and economic migrants from the less fortunate regions.

There has been much talk of the meaning of citizenship — a term used to describe the relationship between the individual and the state in which there are considered to be reciprocal rights and duties. It is often considered that governments have a responsibility to treat each citizen's fate as equally important regardless of religion, gender, age or ethnicity. But the citizen is expected to show various virtues. William Galston, for example, proposes four sorts of civic virtue: social (e.g. open mindedness), political (e.g. political involvement and a respect for the rights of others), economic (e.g. adaptability, a work ethic and the capacity to delay self-gratification) and general (e.g. courage, loyalty and respect for the law). The sort of 'virtuous citizen' who emerges from this formula seems to be rather an old fashioned figure; one that would be entirely acceptable to a decent Victorian capitalist (Galston 1991). Other citizenship theorists have proposed a slightly different list of political virtues; for example, the willingness to listen, to question political authority and to engage in reasonable protest and debate. These sound somewhat more in tune with modern *deliberative democracy*. A willingness to set forth one's views, to accept diversity of opinion and to compromise, are all manifestations of what has been called *public reasonableness*.

Improved mass education, instant communications and a belief in the individual have perhaps made citizens more tolerant of each other while becoming less tolerant of the authority of the state. Kymlicka argues that this growing interest in civic virtues among political philosophers is matched by a growing fear that these virtues are in fact in decline in modern societies which manifest 'greater apathy, passivity and withdrawal into the private sphere' (Kymlicka 2002). A school of thought known as *civic republicanism* has sprung up to address this phenomenon. Civic republicans downplay the value of private life while extolling the value of participation in public duties. They tend to see political life, as Aristotle did, as being on a higher level than private social life. They oppose those modern cynics who are inclined to view politics merely as a disreputable but necessary means to private happiness—a process tarnished by media spin doctors, secretive bureaucrats, power mad politicians and self-interested money-makers. All that is required, so the cynics argue, is that citizens should respect the law, vote at elections and not interfere with the private pleasures of others. The word *civility* has been revived to describe some of these virtues, notwithstanding the danger that this term may put too much emphasis upon the importance of politeness and docility leading to subservience and the toleration of injustice.

All this talk of virtues seems quite interesting but rather facile. Anyone can reel off a list of what they consider to be desirable personal qualities. But on what grounds? Surely a virtue has to be justified in terms of more basic ethical theory or in terms of demonstrable benefits to others. Civility may well be a good thing under certain circumstances but those prescribing it should be able to explain why and when this is the case. Virtue theory tends to concentrate attention upon the good citizen while ignoring the unfortunate victim and, when combined with a communitarian view, this tendency is likely to be accentuated.

All successful states are becoming more multicultural. Like magnets they attract the discontented and ambitious of the world. The result is that many societies become characterised by diversity and cultural pluralism. While liberals have approved of such diversity and exercised toleration, some traditional conservatives have argued that cultural pluralism undermines the traditional values and stability of a common culture.

For more than a hundred years liberal societies have tried to practise toleration and respect for cultural and other group differences. In the United States, wave after wave of immigrants were admitted during the nineteenth and early twentieth centuries and, eventually, became Americans. To do so fully they had to speak English and recognise, formally or informally, the basic ideas of democracy and individual freedom; 'citizenship tests' for such qualities seem to be a good idea. Assimilation was a remarkable achievement by the United States and depended, to an extent, upon the genuine economic opportunities available to immigrants which allowed them to 'better themselves'. America, like some other countries, indulged half-consciously in a process of nation-building by promoting among immigrants a common language and a sense of belonging to a community with certain rights and privileges. Yet, as Charles Taylor notes (Taylor 1997) such nation-building was also to the advantage of those in the majority culture.

Britain faces these problems today. Should British society be entirely multicultural and expect no real integration by immigrant groups? Or should the state encourage, or even insist upon integration? A compromise may be the answer: perhaps social, political and economic integration should be encouraged while artistic and private cultural differences tolerated and, even, celebrated. History suggests that culturally-exclusive education should not be permitted, nor should any form of exclusivity that encourages the formation of ethnic, religious or linguistic ghettoes or stereotypes. Sectarian schools and schools where the teaching itself is conducted in a foreign language should not be licensed. Requirements that immigrants understand the elements of their new country's history, culture, language and laws should be expected; proficiency in the parent language should be emphasised. In this way, the movements of peoples over the face of the globe can become mutually advantageous, the security and good governance of a country like Britain being traded for the energy and commercial enterprise of newcomers. From this, both sides can benefit.

Environmentalism

In order to survive we need an enjoyable and useful environment. If our environment cannot provide what we need and desire then our happiness will be affected.

The 1960s saw a resurgence of awareness of the importance of the environment in our daily lives. Pollution, human overpopulation and resource shortages became political issues. Moderate reformers were dubbed *environmentalists* while radicals were sometimes called *ecologists*. Whereas *shallow ecologism* is anthropocentric in outlook, *deep ecologism* accords value and priority to the planet itself and to the ecosystem which links the whole of the inanimate and animate worlds. Various strains of ecologism emerged, such as eco-feminism (which sees the male sex as the chief origin of environmental damage), eco-anarchism (promoting the idea that the environment, if unmolested, will reach its own equilibrium) and eco-socialism (which ascribes most environmental destruction to capitalism). What can be called *heritage ecologism* harks back to nationalistic roots such as in the Nazi ideas of 'blood and soil', promoting the destruction of what are considered to be foreign plants, animals and artifacts. Because all forms of environmentalism and ecologism seem to imply restrictions on economic growth they have enjoyed only limited governmental support in affluent democracies and outright opposition from some governments of developing nations. Nevertheless, environmentalism and ecologism continue to raise political discourse a little above the immediate and monotonous concerns of materialism and have encouraged the consideration of a more global and long term perspective.

I have elsewhere described seven main forms of environmentalism and ecologism based upon their principal motivations (Ryder 1992). These are the *thrifty*, the *aesthetic*, the *scientific*, the *historic*, the *health-conscious*, the *compassionate* and the *mystical* forms of environmentalism. Each is driven by a typical concern, respectively, to conserve resources (e.g. the claims of biodiversity), to protect beauty, to protect items of scientific or historic interest, to protect health, to avoid causing suffering to any painient being and to respect the integrity of the whole eco-system. The first five of these positions are clearly anthropocentric. That is to say, human benefits are being sought. The sixth, the *compassionate*, extends the moral circle to include all painient individuals, nonhuman as well as human (Ryder 1992) whereas the last, the *mystical*, gives priority to the eco-system of the whole planet, whether painient or not, and even to the whole cosmos. Aldo Leopold, for example, exemplified this *deep ecological* position when he emphasised the paramount significance of the *biotic community*, as he called it, and the need to preserve its 'integrity, stability and beauty' (Leopold 1949). For Leopold, parts of nature have a value independent of their human (or even nonhuman) usefulness.

Some of the confusions in environmental and ecology theory stem from this plethora of moral priorities. Often the theories have been poorly thought out. Sometimes they conflict one with another. These problems have not facilitated the adoption of environmental principles and policies by the political community. Perhaps it would help to define clearly which of the four underlying moral theories is being advocated, whether it is the concern for all *painient* things (painism), for *life* itself (including trees and other plants that are usually considered not to be painient), for all *natural* features (including inanimate things like rocks, rivers and mountains) or a concern that also includes some *human-made things* (like art and buildings). These moral positions are not, of course, mutually exclusive. Indeed, painism encompasses the other three because any damage, for example, to trees, mountains or beautiful buildings (although none of those things are painient), is likely to cause suffering to humans or nonhumans indirectly, and so becomes of very legitimate concern (Ryder 1992). It has been suggested that the relative failure of environmentalism to influence the governments of the world, and particularly that of George W Bush's super-power America, (e.g. its failure to sign the Kyoto Convention) may have helped to spark the current interest in citizenship and in the responsibility of each individual to live a personal lifestyle that is eco-friendly, on the one hand, while, on the other, supporting the establishment of new global structures to protect the world environment (Kymlicka 2002). Global warming and the need to develop non-polluting sources of energy are clearly issues of the gravest urgency.

Human Rights and Duties

If there was a moral basis for politics in the late twentieth century it was the doctrine of rights (see pp. 5–6, 70). Like its classic forebears (equality, liberty and justice) the concept of rights, so I believe, is merely a means to an end, which is increased happiness. By not recognising this, rights theory often gets into trouble, particularly when it comes to clashes between conflicting rights or between rights-holders. There is also much confusion about the meaning of the word 'rights' itself. Many different terms are used. *Legal rights* are those that are enshrined in law. *Moral rights* are those defended on moral grounds. Moral rights, therefore, tend to become legal rights through the processes of political and legislative action. Many such rights are now laid down in international conventions and treaties (see Introduction). Various subtypes of rights have been proposed, Wesley Hohfeld (1879–1918), for example, proposing a quadripartite system of *claim* rights to x (where others have a duty not to interfere with my right to x or even have a duty to assist me), *privilege or liberty* rights to x (where others have no claim rights against this), *power* rights (where I have the power to impinge upon others) and *immunity* rights (where I am freed from the power rights of others). Distinctions have been proposed between *positive rights* (to do x) and *negative rights* (to not do x), and between *active rights* (to do x) and *passive rights* (to not have x done to me). Because it is usually possible to use language in either its active or passive forms to express the same or similar meanings, these distinctions, however, are not always clear, useful or significant.

Human rights were once said to be rights to which human beings are entitled simply because they are human. John Locke proposed the basic human rights of 'life, liberty and property' and Thomas Jefferson the more inspiring trio of 'life, liberty and the pursuit of happiness'. Such rights are often considered to be fundamental, universal and absolute; *fundamental* in the sense that this moral entitlement cannot be removed; *universal* in that they can be claimed by *all* humans everywhere; and *absolute* in the sense that they cannot be reduced or qualified.

The origin of rights is claimed either to be God (in the case of so-called *natural rights*) or the human mind. In general, rights are reputed to 'trump' all other considerations by erecting morally insuperable protective barriers around individuals or groups. Whereas Utilitarianism, for example, is flexible in permitting certain otherwise wrong actions on the grounds that they produce benefits to A that outweigh the costs to B, Rights Theory often dictates a more rigid approach which tends to deny that benefits to A can *ever* outbalance the costs to B. When one set of human rights conflict with another set of human rights, there can be problems; for example, the conflict between the right to self-defence and the right to life, when A attacks B and B resorts to lethal resistance.

In general, rights-language is most comfortably used in those Western societies that have had experience of revolution in the last

250 years and, characteristically, rights-language is the language of the underdog. It forms the slogans of the colonially oppressed, the rebel, the victim and the slave. Only since the United Nations Declaration of Human Rights in 1948 and the European Convention on Human Rights of 1953 have British governments again generally accepted the use of this terminology in the gradual establishment of international law based upon the ideals of liberal democracy. In Britain, the word 'rights' had come into popular use in the seventeenth century (e.g. in the Declaration of Rights of 1689) but, by the nineteenth, was often regarded with distaste, possibly as a reaction against its utilisation as a slogan by French and American revolutionaries. Yet it had been an Englishman, Thomas Paine, whose *The Rights of Man* (1791) had helped establish its use around the world.

Talk of human rights has, now, in many respects, superceded and incorporated the discussion of the more ancient concepts of equality, freedom and justice. While Marxists have openly rejected the idea of rights on the grounds that it protects property (and have covertly resented its implied threat to the power of the state), conservatives have tended to reject rights language in preference for the use of the concept of *duty*. Even in the twenty-first century, among British conservatives, the use of 'duty' is preferred to 'rights', apparently on the grounds that a demand for *rights* is dimly associated with sponging and a grasping dependency, whereas *duty* smacks of nobility of character. For one Labour politician, David Blunkett, the term 'rights' was associated with selfishness while the concept of 'duties' was seen as denoting altruism. Such feelings stem from a long British puritanical tradition that has highly valued self-help and fortitude in the face of adversity. Its downside—a contempt for the underdog—is not so readily admitted. In any case, it seems that the tendency, in some circles, to reject the concept of *rights* in favour of the concept of *duty* usually has an emotional rather than a rational basis. The two concepts are, or should be, merely two sides of the same coin. Those opposed to the concept of 'rights' often assume, wrongly, that the term is being used selfishly. Correspondingly, they assume, too, that 'duty' is always being used unselfishly. This, of course, is not necessarily the case. They are correct, however, in believing that the locus ('me' or 'others') is crucial. Morality is essentially about unselfishness: it deals with what I do for others. Nevertheless, the false argument is often heard to the effect that animals can have no rights because they can exercise no duties (Garner 1993). Such a restriction of rights only to those who can observe duties, would also exclude from the possession of rights all human babies, extremely handicapped adults, those in a coma and those who are suffering from advanced dementia. This line of argument seems to be based upon the confused notion that the term *rights* is being used only to signify *active, positive* or *power rights* rather than *passive rights*—and, in particular, the most important right of all that embraces all others—*the passive right not to be caused pain.*

Jeremy Bentham famously rejected the concept of *natural rights* as 'nonsense upon stilts', although this was not a rejection of the idea of rights itself, as is sometimes claimed, but of the notion that rights have a natural or divine origin. Today, it is generally accepted among secular philosophers that a right is simply a human invention.

The word 'duty' is only slightly older than the word 'right' and was, so it seems, originally used to indicate homage or respect for a feudal superior. A little later it was used synonymously with the word 'debt'. 'Due' was used as a noun, in the sixteenth century, in the sense that we refer to a passive right today, just as the word 'libertie' was used for an active right. Traditionally, therefore, and even in the writings of philosophers until Kant, *duty and obligation* implied being subject to the will of another person, such as a feudal lord or creditor, who has the authority and power to impose penalties in the case of the non-fulfilment of a duty. In contrast, Immanuel Kant (1724–1804) argued that duty is the necessity to act in a certain way that springs from the demands of reason alone. Kant saw duty as a requirement that is binding on everyone *regardless of their inclinations*. So he rejected David Hume's ideas that the passions dominate reason and that duty is a kind of sentiment. For Kant, control of the self seemed to be of paramount importance. His Lutheran background supported his belief in firm self-discipline and in the suppression of sexual and other feelings. This rigid control of spontaneous impulses is the psychological key to understanding Kant's philosophy. Kant and Hume are not really incompatible on the origins of goodness, as they are usually regarded as being. An identical act of comfort or caring, for example, can spring equally from either a calculated and rational (Kantian) sense of duty or from a more spontaneous and emotional (Humean) *instinct of compassion*. Indeed, very often it can spring from both duty and compassion at the same time. A rational sense of right and wrong is, however, required to distinguish between positive impulses and hurtful ones, liberating the former while restraining the latter.

'Duty' has, unfortunately, become a catch-phrase for religious traditionalists ranging from Tony Blair to the American Neo-Conservatives, some of whom believe that liberalism is selfish, individualistic
and decadent. Like some Moslem fundamentalists the Neo-Conservatives seek 'moral regeneration'. Together, they attacked the forces
of the USSR in Afghanistan in the 1990s. Some follow the obscure
Leo Strauss in maintaining that there is one kind of truth for the
masses and another for themselves. They see religion as a useful
myth for subordinating others; a 'noble lie' for maintaining social
order (Singer 2004). Neo-Conservatism appears to be more of a cult
than a true philosophy. It is patriotic and elitist and smacks of paranoia, but otherwise seems strangely lacking in content. Ultimately, it
appears to be based upon a deep-seated fear of sexual freedom and
'moral decline'. Yet, hypocritically, Neo-Conservatives have pre-
sided over the erosion of values associated with the use of abhorrent
weapons in the Iraq war, and the mistreatment and torture of prisoners in Guantanamo.

Some Christian fundamentalists are in a similar position. They
fear what would happen if their own impulses, sexual and aggressive, were given full reign. They project this fear onto society at large
and so imagine that society is in decline and on the brink of deca-
dence and disintegration. Sadly, instead of addressing the real moral
challenges of the world today, many Christians continue to work
themselves into a lather about harmless issues such as gay marriage
and women priests. Pope Benedict is one of the worst offenders. The
obsession with sex still stifles the Roman Catholic Church, where
male priests appear to fiddle while the world burns. They seem to
ignore poverty, torture and the abrogation of human rights while
disproportionately parading their prejudices against homosexual-
ity. For this reason, the church has become absurd in the eyes of
many: a pathetic travesty of the teachings of Jesus. Jesus today
would be working for Médicin Sans Frontières, Amnesty International or the Red Cross.

Animal Rights

The proposal to extend the concept of rights, and indeed, moral status generally, to animals, is not new. References can be found in the
seventeenth century and by the eighteenth, even Jeremy Bentham
(who disliked the claim that rights have a 'natural' or divine origin)
urged that animals should be given rights:

> The day may come when the rest of the animal creation may
> acquire those rights which never could have been withheld from
> them but by the hand of tyranny ... (Bentham 1780).

John Stuart Mill concurred and urged governments to intervene to
protect animals from cruelty. They were, he said, in a similar moral
position to children.

In the twentieth century the issue was revived by members of the
informal Oxford Group[1] (Ryder 1970). Brigid Brophy, Ruth Harrison, Andrew Linzey, Stanley and Roslind Godlovitch, John Harris,
David Wood and myself were all involved in the publication of *Animal Men and Morals* in 1971 and we were fortunate that both Peter
Singer (from Australia) and Tom Regan (from the United States)
were passing through Oxford at that time. Singer became involved
and carried the revival across the Atlantic by publishing his magisterial *Animal Liberation* in New York in 1975 although, as a Utilitarian,
he eschewed the formal use of the concept of *rights* in favour of Utilitarian terminology and the employment of my concept of *speciesism*.
Tom Regan's classic exposition was *The Case for Animal Rights* published in 1983. My own leaflet *Speciesism* appeared in 1970, *Victims of
Science* was published in 1975 and my *Animal Revolution : Changing
Attitudes Towards Speciesism* in 1989.

To an extent, twentieth-century anti-speciesists were drawing
attention to the implications of Darwinism — and were supported by
Richard Dawkins in doing so (Dawkins 1976). The argument went
like this: if humans are related biologically through evolution to the
other animals then, surely, we should also be related morally. There
should be no great moral divide between ourselves and the other
animals. Science, after all, has produced increasing anatomical, biochemical and behavioural evidence that many other animals can
also suffer pain, fear, boredom and other forms of distress.

From the 1970s onwards, European and English-speaking legislatures began to recognise this logic with the passage of more protective legislation to restrain the worst abuses found in modern
laboratories, factory farms and elsewhere. Major campaigns were
fought to protect apes, whales, seals, elephants, exported live food
animals, cruelly trapped animals and hunted prey. Public support
for such campaigns flourished most in societies that were both affluent and peaceful. In political terms, the European movement
advanced more rapidly than the American. British governments, in

---

[1]   Not to be confused with the extreme right wing 'moral rearmament'
      tendency that is sometimes given the same name.

particular, were obliged to listen to the scientific and legal arguments of lobbyists and to respect the growing evidence that votes could be harvested from emotive issues of this character (Ryder 1998).

Increasing interest in animal protection began to be shown in academic circles in the 1980s, where its politics, history, law, ethics and, above all, the science of animal welfare, began to be recognised as subjects worthy of study (Ryder 1975, 1989, 1998; Radford 2001; Broom & Johnson 1993; Webster 1994). By the end of the century most professional ethicists supported the general thesis that the prejudice of speciesism is wrong. For them, and for political philosophers, it is a challenge to face up to the full implications of extending the scope of their traditionally anthropocentric deliberations so as to include other painient species, and to recognise an issue that has already become a political and electoral reality, particularly in affluent and peaceful states (Ryder 2003, 2004).

Terrorism

The United Nations' definition of 'terrorism' covers all actions aimed at killing innocent civilians for political purposes. Arguably, this also covers the actions of states where, as in Iraq, during the waging of war, innocent civilians are killed. The intentions may differ, but the known consequences are the same. There is no agreement as to why a state, democratic or not, should have greater moral authority for committing acts of violence than does an individual.

Political violence, including terrorism, has two main components:

1. External causes such as political oppression, threat or injustice.

2. Individuals who react strongly to these causes by taking violent action.

In order to understand terrorism fully both components, the political reality and the psychology of the individual, need to be studied. It is the interaction of these two components that leads to political violence.

In the case of so-called 'Islamic terrorism' the external political causes are plain to see: the material and political ascendancy of the West, widespread oppression and bad governance in North Africa and the Middle East, and, in particular, the political cancers of Palestine, Iraq, Afghanistan and Chechenya, for all of which the West (or Russia), partly or wholly, are held responsible. The outrages perpetrated by ill-disciplined US forces in the Abu Ghraib and Guantanamo prisons have made the situation far worse and helped to pin the blame more securely upon the West.

Much analysis has been carried out on these political causes. The West has been implicated, realistically, because of its active roles in instigating and supporting the modern state of Israel, launching the Afghan and Iraq wars of the twenty-first century, and for its tacit support of corrupt and oppressive Islamic regimes. Paradoxically, the West is also blamed for *not interfering more* in bringing justice and peace in Israel and elsewhere. For some young Muslims, the West is viewed as an all powerful but uncaring father who has ignored the sufferings of his children. It has been suggested that only about one per cent of adult members of all Islamic societies react to the political realities by becoming involved in or strongly supportive of active terrorism. What, then, are the psychological characteristics of this group? Who are the particularly susceptible individuals who typically become violent political activists?

Throughout history, so it seems, many revolutionaries, terrorists and freedom fighters have shared certain psychological features. There are two main psychological types: first, there are the *pioneers*, those who are individually motivated. These are often socially isolated, intelligent and thoughtful people. They are not mentally ill but they burn with the anger that is frequently to be found in young men. The anger is in fact partly caused, or at least intensified, by feelings of rejection, frustration, or insult within their personal lives — from their family members or their peers. The pioneers are often loners (although sometimes with a sociable persona) who feel deeply unaccepted and resentful. They usually, but not always, see themselves as failures. They may have been bullied or isolated at school or at work, or may have been harshly disciplined by their fathers. Typically, they seek an external explanation for their feelings in the wider social and political context. They identify with the victims of oppression and project their personal problems onto the world at large, displacing their anger onto figures of political authority or onto social structures (the 'state', the 'bourgeoisie' or 'the West') or at social situations or ideas ('racism', discrimination or religious prejudice). Frequently, they distort or misinterpret the causes of their malaise, seeing only the political causes.

The second group, who are more numerous than the pioneers, are the *followers*. These are often young people looking for excitement and a meaning to their lives, who can easily be led. They seek the approval of those around them. They conform to their immediate subculture.

They are less thoughtful and even more psychologically 'normal' than the pioneers. Most young people in all societies are vulnerable to indoctrination by peers or adults. Most want to prove themselves in some way. Most crave attention, fame or even notoriety. Most seek a firm sense of identity and esteem. By joining a gang, a team or a movement the followers can achieve these aims and feel fulfilled.

Of course, a few terrorists will fall into neither classification and many will fall into both. Neither group are particularly able to empathise with other people; such feelings are suppressed by their feelings of anger.

The backgrounds of the London suicide bombers of 7 July 2005 have received a great deal of attention. One, Mohammad Sidique Khan, was aged 30, and, superficially, appeared to be integrated into life in Leeds, becoming a classroom monitor in a primary school. But he also worked in an Islamic bookshop and had had many contacts with radical Islamic groups in Britain and abroad. It was said that he had few friends in his neighbourhood and was described as being 'quiet'. Although born in Leeds Khan had visited Pakistan on several occasions. A university graduate, he lived in a community where there was much support for the racist far Right among white voters. Shehzad Tanweer, aged 22, born in Bradford, also appeared westernised. Like Khan he, too, was described as 'quiet' and 'polite'. His interest had been in cricket and other sports although he had been good at school work and was described as 'super intelligent'. His friends had noticed that he was becoming increasingly religious. He, too, had visited Pakistan in the year previous to the bombings. Hasib Mir Hussain, aged 18, was different from his friends Khan and Tanweer in that he was a failure at school work. As a boy in Bradford he was described as 'quieter' and more reserved than his older brother. Like Khan and Tanweer he had visited Pakistan shortly prior to the bombings and returned far more interested in religion. A cousin remarked, 'I thought he had been brainwashed.'

The first two, Khan and Tanweer, clearly fall into the pioneer category and Khan was almost certainly their leader. The third, Hasib Mir Hussain, was rather less of a pioneer and may have followed the lead of the other two. None had had much worldly success, all were described as 'quiet', and all had become noticeably more religious after recent visits to Pakistan. All had grown up in a part of England where overt racial prejudice was endemic and where the slogan 'PAKI SCUM' was commonplace. Two of these bombers were identified when their concerned families reported them missing to the police after the bombings in London. The fourth bomber, also their friend, came from a black West Indian background. Born in Jamaica, Germaine Lindsay, aged 19, had recently converted to Islam. He had been brought up in Huddersfield and educated in a largely white class at Rawthorpe High School. He was keen on martial arts, was recently married and had moved to Aylesbury where he did not mix with his neighbours. It is difficult to classify him as either a pioneer or a follower but, like Khan and Tanwear, he was academically bright and described as 'a bit of a loner'. He was, therefore, probably more of a pioneer. It is important to realise that all four were close friends: they were loners who had found companionship in terrorism. Loyalty to their ideals was strong.

All four bombers were reported by their associates to feel angered by the foreign policies of Britain and America, especially, as they saw it, by the West's support for Israel's suppression of Palestine and by the invasion of Iraq in 2003. All wanted to see the withdrawal of Western troops from Iraq. Three out of four seemed fairly typical of second-generation Islamic youth in Britain and they had certain shared features: all felt a kinship with the international Islamic community to the extent that they identified themselves with the victims of attacks upon Moslems in Israel and Iraq; all were not fully integrated into British society; all felt some conflict of identity between being Muslim and British; all came from parts of Britain where race relations were bad (unlike in London where they committed their atrocities); all felt cut off from their parents' generation; all were intelligent people who had turned back to their Islamic roots; and none had found ways to express their political concerns through effective and peaceful democratic channels. Indeed, all had witnessed recent so-called democratic elections that had failed to remove the two main architects of the Iraq war — President Bush and Prime Minister Blair. To an extent, all four terrorists had failed to achieve success in competitive Western secular society and so had reverted back to the less challenging and demanding culture of their religion. They had, in their own terrible way, put a twisted morality into their politics.

Just as the personalities of Islamic terrorists need to be understood, so do the personalities of those in the West who were the architects of the Iraq war: warmongering leaders have been all too frequent in the past, from Genghis Khan and Napoleon through to Hitler. What they have in common is that their sense of their own value is associated with successful aggression. Often, they are supremely ambitious. Like some of the pioneer terrorists, some of these men suffered from idolising mothers and oppressive fathers. The idolising mother gives them the lifelong conviction that they are special people, out of the ordinary, 'men of destiny', while the oppressive father supplies them with enduring anger and the model of physical aggression. Feeling unfulfilled as young men they determine to seek power and, when they get it, they use it to prove to themselves (and their mothers) that they really are messiahs, the saviours of their people. They need to reduce the feeling of 'dissonance' between what they are and what they feel they really should be. This is one of the origins of the paranoid personality which is characterised by an exaggerated sense of threat on one hand and a sense of messianic self-importance on the other. Paranoid thinking patterns are relatively common and are not necessarily a sign of serious mental illness. They are, however, a potent danger when found in powerful politicians.

Paranoids are probably attracted to politics in the first place, but to make matters worse, politics often exacerbates their paranoid condition. Possible paranoid features can be seen in the case of Tony Blair whose almost delusionary sense of persecution was exemplified in his persistent belief in the threat to the UK posed by weapons of mass destruction (WMD) in the absence of, or despite, the evidence. In addition to such persecutory fantasies the paranoid typically shows a sense of messianic mission. Both Blair and Bush have demonstrated this in their excited rush to war and in their grandiose statements in their own defence. The religious tinge to their thinking, too, is consistent, as is their general dramatising of the importance of the terrorist threat. Yet, paranoids are notoriously good at appearing to be normal; they erect convincing schemes to explain their dangerous behaviour, despite fatal flaws in the premises upon which their arguments are based. The paranoid's overwhelming sense of self-importance and infallibility blinds them to the possibility that they may be wrong. Typically, the paranoid externalises and puts the blame upon others while finding 'high-minded' external or divine justifications for their own, sometimes homicidal, actions. Whatever destruction they cause they continue to see themselves as saviours. The West has taken a long time to wake up to the fact that Bush and Blair, urging each other on in a classic paranoid *folie à deux*, have caused massive moral and physical damage.

Since the Pinochet judgement in 1998 national courts have had a role in the prosecution of the most serious international crimes, among these being the waging of illegal war. It can no longer be assumed that immunities will be accorded to (former) heads of state or ministers (Heywood 2000; Sands 2003). Indeed, those who have been responsible for initiating policies are now deemed most culpable. Instead of reducing the threat of terrorism by dealing with its material causes — most notably the oppression of the Palestinians — Bush and Blair took action that, predictably, made matters a lot worse, killed thousands of innocent civilians and exposed their own peoples to an increased threat of terrorist attack.

If political violence is to be curtailed, its root causes, both psychological and political, need to be addressed. Terrorism has, of course, prompted new anti-terrorism legislation which in some cases itself threatens civil liberties and is, itself, provocative. The right of the individual to feel safe often conflicts with her right not to be arrested arbitrarily, or even to be shot by ill-trained police upon mere suspicion. The threat posed by terrorism is matched by the threat of the state. In a democracy, Parliament, and not the executive, must decide where to draw the lines between protecting the innocent civilian from being killed or wounded by terrorists on one hand and the possibility of being imprisoned or shot by the state on the other. Neither threat should be underestimated. To wound someone with a bomb will, almost certainly, cause agony and enduring harm. But, equally, to imprison a person unjustly, even for a few weeks, may cause lasting harm in terms of psychological health, reputation, relationships and career. It may also turn a good citizen into an embittered and dangerous person who is more likely to become a terrorist. In general, draconian measures should only be passed with built-in deadlines that indicate when they will automatically expire. *Suffering and death caused by the state are no less serious moral matters, indeed, possibly more so, than when caused by terrorists.* (The British police shoot and kill two or three persons a year without ever being convicted of an offence, even manslaughter. Surely police should be *more* culpable, not less.) To deprive an individual of her rights on the grounds that this *may* in the future be to the convenience or safety of a larger number of people is wrong on two counts: it is putting *uncertain* future effects ahead of present pains that are *certain*, and making the convenience or safety of the *many* more important than the suffering of the *one*.

Perhaps the greatest harm done by terrorism is that it puts itself at the centre of the political stage. In doing so, it distracts political attention away from more important matters such as poverty, sickness and oppression; the weakest and most vulnerable individuals in our world become increasingly ignored. Paradoxically, terrorism can thus distract attention away from its own causes.

Good Governance

Terrorism is often the pursuit of a just grievance through immoral means. So, the grievance needs to be recognised and addressed while the violent means are suppressed. Often, terrorism is rebellion against bad governance. The techniques of good governance are, therefore, of great importance, and have been improved in recent decades, particularly in the West. I believe that basing politics upon science and open morality should be among the basic skills deployed. There are, of course, many other components of good governance that are beyond the scope of this book. Fundamental are the skills of good economic management, the delivery of good educational and health services, the provision of full employment and the other genuine benefits of democracy. Both Britain and the US, however, lay themselves open to the charge of hypocrisy on the question of democracy. How can they preach democracy to the world when they, themselves, are not true democracies? The lack of proportional representation, the distortions caused by money, patronage, spin and the party whip system are glaring faults. These will have to be put right before either the US or Britain can be taken seriously on the subject of democracy.

Until the latter half of the twentieth century, it was widely considered that moral considerations were inappropriate in international affairs (Brown 1993). Foreign policies were expected to be determined entirely by national interests, and the dictatorships of the twentieth century encouraged a cynical 'real politik' that power alone mattered. Such so-called *realism* only began to be challenged after World War Two (Beitz 1979). International law is now moving on and certain moral imperatives are, rightly, considered to transcend national boundaries. What, after all, is so imperative about geography? Suffering is global (Dunne & Wheeler 1999). Is there not a moral obligation on well-governed democratic nations to help other nations to achieve good governance?

All these contemporary issues have raised the question — what, ultimately, should politics be aiming for? What is the underlying moral objective? Each issue gives glimpses of what the answer might be. None of the traditional political ideals, however, provides a satisfactory moral basis for politics today.

PART II

Putting Morality Into Politics

I'm all for codes of conduct
Richard Dawkins, BBC World, 20 April 2004

In Part I we looked at some of the main issues in politics today and such underlying principles as justice, freedom, equality and democracy. Sometimes, as we have seen, these principles are mutually incompatible, and they certainly do not form consistent or universal moral theories upon which policies can easily be based. Let us, then, examine some other moral positions as possible candidates.

Aristotle, at least, saw the importance of happiness (*eudaimonia*) — attained through moderation and reason. He also argued a continuity between ethics and politics and he advocated constitutional government. He was, however, an unashamed elitist and excluded women, children, slaves, animals and foreigners from serious moral consideration. Kant promoted the idea of duty and advocated acting according to universal rules, showing respect for persons and never treating others as a means but always also as an end in themselves. Kant despised pragmatism. He also proposed that states should enter into a permanent agreement never to use force. Kant's emphasis was upon duty itself, however, rather than its effects, and he failed to specify what duties were good or to see the ultimate importance of happiness or compassion. Like many who emphasise the importance of duty Kant had a fear and dislike of sexuality, seeing it as 'a degradation of humanity'(Wood 2001). David Hume is one of the first to see the importance of compassion and argues that it is only such feelings that can move us to action. Reason must be their slave, he said. Moral ideas are the expression of feelings that arise in us because we must cooperate to survive. He did not, however, describe how feelings of anger and aggression should be handled. Jeremy Bentham, one of the fathers of Utilitarianism, argued that the proper moral objective is to achieve 'the greatest happiness of the greatest number', including in this calculus both foreigners and animals. Bentham rejected what he saw as the fictions of so-called moral contracts and moral rights. Not only were they figments of human imagination, he argued, but the idea of rights had led to the horrors of the French Revolution. Nevertheless, Bentham believed that Utilitarianism could form a rational foundation for politics, although he did not convincingly explain how the aggregated pleasures of the majority could justify the oppression of the few.

I would suggest that none of these approaches in themselves, except possibly Bentham's, provide enough detail or precision to constitute a sound moral basis for politics today.

Are there then any moral foundations on which we can all agree, at least to some extent? I believe there are and that they are these: *pain is bad*, and so, *causing unnecessary pain to others is wrong.* To say that pain is bad is almost stating the obvious. Indeed, badness and pain are often synonymous. Bad, quite simply, can mean painful. If one lists all the traditional sins or vices, such as greed, lust, envy, injustice, ire or intemperance, and asks what they all have in common it is that they are likely to cause pain (broadly defined) to others. Conversely, those qualities or ideals that are considered good are likely to cause pleasure (or pain reduction) to others: liberty, justice, brotherhood and equality, for example, or virtues such as mercy, fairness, generosity, truthfulness and benevolence. They are all means to this same end. We do not usually ask 'why is pain a bad thing?' or 'why is happiness good?' These things are self-evident. Good things are all qualities we seek for ourselves: that is basic psychology. The moral step comes when we strive to supply these good things to *others*. When we try to do to others what we believe will reduce their pains or increase their pleasures and make them happy, then we are doing moral good.

For centuries pain was strangely ignored by philosophers. Perhaps this was because it was accepted that pain was inextricably a part of life and nothing much could be done about it—best then to try to ignore it (Ryder 1998). Modern psychology generally supports the Benthamite view that pain-reductions and pleasures are important ingredients of happiness (Argyle 1987), although there is no suggestion that happiness is simply an individual's sum of pleasures. Contentment is more like a mood that settles over our experiences: if we are happy we can take some pains in our stride, but if we are sad then nothing seems to be pleasurable. Yet there is a strong positive correlation between painful experiences and unhappiness. A loss, for example, (of job, spouse or assets) can precipitate a depressed mood that may last for months. Chronic physical pains can have a similar effect. Conversely, successes often cause happiness. But happiness and unhappiness are still hard to pin down. Pain seem to be more specific and measurable.

Utilitarianism

Several moral theories have explicitly recognised pain as the only evil. As we have seen, British Utilitarian philosophers such as Jeremy Bentham and John Stuart Mill regarded pain and pleasure as the basic ingredients of happiness, and they saw happiness as the foundation of morality. 'Actions', said Mill 'are right in proportion as they tend to promote happiness, wrong as they tend to promote the reverse of happiness'. Mill's version of Utilitarianism, however, recognised superior and inferior *qualities* of pleasures ('better a Socrates dissatisfied than a pig satisfied') whereas Bentham was concerned to measure happiness strictly in terms of *quantities* of pain and pleasure ('other things being equal, pushpin is as good as poetry'). Utilitarianism still underlies modern economic planning where the assumptions are made that pain-reduction is equivalent to pleasure and that happiness can be measured in economic terms. Basically, Bentham's form of Utilitarianism proposes that an action is right if and only if it will produce more total pleasure or happiness, or be more preventative of total pain or unhappiness, than any alternative action, *where pains and pleasures are totalled or aggregated across all those individuals (including animals) affected by the action*. Making calculations of this sort are clearly difficult. Bentham suggested that pains and pleasures should be measured according to their intensity, duration, propinquity, fecundity (the chance that a pain or pleasure is followed by others), purity (the chance that a pain or pleasure is followed by its opposite) and extent (the numbers of individuals affected). He proposed that this 'hedonic calculus' should form the basis not only for morality generally, but also for criminal law. Subsequent writers have simplified this calculus to the aggregation of pains and pleasures of all those affected by an action over a specified time, where equal quantities of pain and pleasure (benefits and costs) are considered to cancel one another.

The tendency to ridicule such calculations on the grounds of their impracticality may not have taken into account the current and future potential of cognitive science. Widely different qualities of pains and pleasures may all register in certain systems of the brain merely according to their 'hedonistic intensity', that is to say the intensity of their pleasurableness or painfulness, and it may, one day, become possible objectively to measure the activities of these systems. We all, in effect, already do this subjectively whenever we compare and rate our own pains and pleasures when establishing preferences and in making decisions generally.

Bentham advocated Utilitarianism as a practical method for making both private and political decisions. His theory became a driving force behind early nineteenth-century reform in Britain, affecting the treatment of tenants and employees, the regulation of public health and, eventually, changes in the social security system. The influence of Utilitarianism remains strong to this day and is seen in the use of the concepts of cost benefit analysis, marginal utility and welfare economics. The word 'utility' is often employed instead of the word 'happiness'—an example of how political philosophers tend to feel so embarrassed by the concept of happiness that it rarely appears even in the index of books on political philosophy. Helvétius and the Utilitarians dared to rediscover happiness as well as pain and pleasure, in the eighteenth century but, among philosophers, these topics have, today, all but disappeared again.

There are two main problems with Utilitarianism: the first is purely procedural—how to measure happiness (utility). The second is far more serious and it is this: Utilitarians habitually add up the happinesses (or the pains and pleasures) of those individuals affected by an action. So if action A causes 10 units of happiness to one person and 20 units to another, its total score is said to be 30 units of happiness, and it is thus considered morally superior to action B if B causes a total, among all those individuals affected by it, of only, say, 15 units of happiness. Furthermore, most Utilitarians see no problem in balancing unhappiness (or pain) scores against happiness (or pleasure) scores in order to achieve grand totals. So if action C causes 5 units of unhappiness to Bob and 10 units of unhappiness to Sally but 100 units of happiness each to Michael and Delia, then it is considered a morally good action because the total of happiness (200 units) outweighs the total of unhappiness (15 units).

Clearly, this habit of aggregating happiness and unhappiness, or pleasures and pains, can lead to some very disturbing results. Imagine a gang of ten sadists who torture a prisoner severely causing the victim 100 units of pain. Even if the sadists only experience an average 20 units of pleasure each, according to most versions of Utilitarianism their outrageous action is still morally right because it causes a total of 200 units of pleasure (i.e. 10 x 20) — thereby outweighing very considerably the victim's pain (100 units). Like democracy, Utilitarianism can clearly be bad news for minorities and for individuals. This habit of totalling pains and pleasures across individuals is one of the main errors in ethics today. It is wrong because it overlooks the fact that pain, pleasure and happiness are *subjective experiences*. If they are not experienced they are not real. Nobody actually experiences any of the total scores (see pp. 74–77). This is the great mistake of Utilitarian ethics and in the ethics of democracy, too.

Rights Theory

The moral approach that tends to avoid this problem is *Rights Theory* where each individual is said to have rights either to do (or not to do) certain things or to (not) have things done to them. Sometimes these rights are enshrined in law and sometimes they are just on the moral level (see Introduction). In the past, there was a tendency to assume that such rights had an external reality because they were based upon some divine law, but over the last century or so rights have usually been seen as mere human inventions. Talk of 'rights' tends to focus the moral concern upon the experience of the victim, and usually it gives priority to individuals rather than to groups or aggregates of individuals. Certain human rights—to life, liberty and property—have been widely accepted since the days of John Locke (1632–1704). Later, the American Declaration of Independence in 1776 introduced the right to 'the pursuit of happiness' which replaced Locke's right to property. Rights are often regarded as absolute and unyielding, thus being able to 'trump' all other moral considerations. Like all moral theories, however, Rights Theory has to deal with moral conflicts. These are of two sorts: the conflict between the rights of different individuals and the conflict of different rights within one individual. When a conflict of rights occurs some sort of prioritisation of rights or of individuals has to be recognised, and in practice, rights moralists find this embarrassing and difficult. For example, do the rights of women or foreigners count for less than the rights of well educated white males? If so, why? Do the rights of chimpanzees count for still less? Or does a right to liberty count for less than a right to justice or more than a right to a good education? If not, why not? How do we balance the right not to be bombed against the right not to be imprisoned without charge? As I see it, uncertainty as to how to prioritise rights and to trade off the rights of one individual against those of another, are the main problems with Rights Theory. The prioritisation of rights often appears to be arbitrary.

Contractarianism

Contractarianism means thinking of society as if it were set up by a social contract which governs the rules of political action as well as private behaviour. To an extent, Rawls reactivated this approach, deriving the idea from Hobbes, Locke and Rousseau. Contractarianism assumes that if we found ourselves in an anarchic 'state of nature' all rational individuals would choose to create a state to protect our interests. Ultimately, though, contractarians justify the state through its overall benefits to general welfare. Do we then tacitly consent to the authority of the state to tax us or put us in prison merely by accepting its benefits?

Some Problems

We can see that all moral theories have their problems. Religious ones are simply dogmatic and appear increasingly incredible. Kantian theory is vague and underemphasises emotion. Utilitarianism can overlook the interests of minorities and individuals. Contractarianism seems to be based upon a purely hypothetical contract. Virtue Theory is arbitrary and too little concerned with victims generally, while Rights Theory cannot always satisfactorily resolve conflicts between rights. It is hardly surprising that modern ethics is often considered to be problematic and that our society is seen as being morally relativistic, pluralistic and, frankly, morally confused.

A constant difficulty in ethics is the *trade-off problem*: the balancing of the costs and benefits of one individual (or group) against another's. The trade-off problem has to be addressed by every moral theory, and in disciplines such as economics and political science, as well as in everyday life, such cost-benefit analyses are not only standard practice but often the area where most disagreements are to be found. Is it right to build a road across a site of special environmental interest? Is it right to go to war to rescue a country from a dictator? Is it right to beat a child in order to discourage insulting behaviour? All such questions involve the evaluation of costs and benefits and the trade-off between them. The building of the road may have environmental costs but economic advantages. The war will have costs in terms of civilian casualties but benefits, perhaps, in terms of future freedoms or material gains. The pain of punishment to the child has to be balanced against the benefits of better behaviour to others. In each case the strengths of the costs and the benefits have to be estimated and then a balance made. It is a two-stage process. Utilitarianism is strong in this regard because such cost-benefit calculations are at the heart of Utilitarian theory and so they are out in the open. Other approaches tend to blur or conceal the problem. One might argue that the gains of all those using the road, when aggregated, outweigh the pains to those few rabbits, toads and naturalists whose environment is spoiled; that the future pleasures of those enjoying freedom from dictatorship outweigh the pains of those innocents who are bombed when the dictator is overthrown; that the pain of the beaten boy is outbalanced by the reduced pains of all those who would otherwise have been insulted by him. Although Rights Theory pretends to have no truck with such cost-benefit analyses at all it deals with substantially the same issue under the name of 'conflicts of rights'; the right to a decent environment versus the right to a road, the right not to be beaten versus the rights of others not to be insulted; the right not to be imprisoned without charge versus the right not to be bombed by a terrorist.

In ethics we are not dealing with tablets of stone. Nothing is made of granite. But I believe we can try to reach some certainties by clearing away confusions and irrelevancies as far as possible. I hope I am putting forward a moral system that is clear, and which addresses openly three of the four most important problems in ethics — the problems of foundations, aggregations and trade-offs. (The other great problem, that of free-will, is not a problem once one accepts that free will is an illusion and probably based upon the experience of quantum uncertainty — see Ryder 2001.) There seems no good reason why morality should not influence all areas of human life. There should not be one set of moral rules for private life and other sets of rules for politics or war. Different circumstances will demand different responses but these should all be within the same moral framework.

Painism

Painism is based upon the premise that the only bad thing is pain. Of course, pain has its indirect benefits as a danger sign but, of itself, pain is always bad. There is nothing bad that is not painful and nothing painful that is not bad. In this context 'pain' means any form of suffering: sensory, cognitive or emotional (Ryder 2001) and so covers such experiences as fear, boredom and sadness.

The foundations of painism are that:

1. Pain (i.e. suffering) is the only evil.

2. Causing pain to others is, prima facie, wrong.

3. In calculating right and wrong it is meaningless to aggregate the pains (or pleasures) of several individuals because pains are only pains when they are actually experienced, and no individual directly experiences any pains other than his own.

4. It is legitimate to trade off the pains and pleasures of one individual against those of another; this is allowable because both are actual experiences.

We all know that pain (suffering) is a fundamental part of our lives. Every waking moment is spent, instinctively and through experience, avoiding sufferings for ourselves, whether great or small. The higher animals, including humankind, also show an instinct for empathy — the natural tendency to understand that another is suffering and to react to this, at least sometimes, with compassion. The fact that I am basing my moral and political theories upon such universals as pain and empathy means that painism goes with the flow of nature (pp. 42–43, 56). It is an attempt to codify these fundamental aspects of our basic being and so to fortify them against other equally primitive and *opposing* urges that arise from anger, lust or greed. Because painism's psychological foundations are so natural — the experiences of pain and empathy — it can claim a true universality, although painism's 'naturalness' does not, of course, necessarily mean it is valid. Just as nobody pursues happiness in order to find anything other than happiness, so nobody strives to reduce pain in order to reduce anything other than pain. Pain is always at the end of the track: it is the ultimate and essential badness. 'Painful' and 'bad' are synonymous in the mind of the child and, at a basic level, in all our minds.

As we have seen, all behaviours traditionally regarded as morally wrong tend to cause pain — murder, rape, lying, cheating and stealing, for example. What, then, about such great moral principles as liberty, justice and equality that we have been considering? My answer is that these are good precisely because they intend to reduce pain. Not having liberty, or justice or equality can all cause pain (pp. 18–19). Most of the classic virtues tend to have a similar result; wisdom, justice, moderation, courage, magnanimity and so on, all tend to reduce pain. All rights and duties, too, have the same objective; take, for example, the rights to work, equality before the law, education, social security and health care, or the passive rights to freedom from torture, degrading treatment, slavery and discrimination—all these have the effect of reducing and avoiding pain. Pain, in my opinion, is the basis for all these traditional moral concepts. This, in my view, gives painism some claim to be well founded.

Like Utilitarianism, painism's aim is to increase happiness through the reduction of pain. What distinguishes my theory of painism from Utilitarianism is principally that I reject the *aggregation* of several individuals' pains and pleasures when calculating the moral rightness or wrongness of actions. (Paragraph 3 above.) Pain is an *experience*. If we are talking of others' pain then that is only a *report* of pain, it is not real pain because it is not directly experienced. The experience of pain is an essential part of the description of pain. So the aggregations of the pains of separate individuals is a meaningless activity because nobody experiences such aggregations. Consider some other sorts of feelings: if one individual feels 2 degrees of love, for example, and another feels 7 degrees of love, we do not add them up and claim that the total—9 degrees of love—has any great significance. The same applies to feelings of total pain as to feelings of total love. *Nobody actually feels such totals.* So why do Utilitarians regard them as significant morally? Unexperienced pains are only husks—they are merely the *reports* of pain. Yet laws and government policies are still based upon the illusion that it is the *numbers of victims* that matter, rather than the intensity of pain of each individual (non-human as well as human). You may, under some circumstances, justify causing minor suffering to one individual in order to bring far greater benefit to another individual, but you can never rationally *aggregate* the pains and pleasures of many separate individuals in making ethical calculations.

Of course, *within* the same individual, pains and pleasures can be aggregated. If someone punches my jaw and, in consequence, I have a slight toothache (say 2 units of pain) and a lot of anxiety (say, 10 units of pain), then I see no reason why these cannot be aggregated to a total of 12 units of pain. These are all relevant because I am actually *experiencing all* of them. If, when I am punched, I fall onto a dog and break one of its ribs then that dog's pain (say 50 units) can also be taken into account as a consequence of the punch but not added to my pain. Nor can the pain of distress felt by the dog's owner (say 20 units) at seeing her dog injured. Painism is concerned about every individual's pains, including the pains of individuals of other species. Pain is pain regardless as to who or what suffers it. So, painism opposes speciesism. If tomorrow's robots can feel pain then 10 units of a robot's pain counts just the same as 10 units of a dog's pain or 10 units of a human's pain.

If we cannot aggregate all these pains (sufferings) of different individuals, then how do we calculate which actions are morally superior? In painism, I propose we do this by taking into account the total pains of the *maximum sufferer* in each case. In the case we have just been considering I felt a combined pain score of 12 units, the dog felt 50 units and his owner felt 20 units. So in this case it is the dog who is the maximum sufferer. We do not add up all the scores as a Utilitarian would do (12 + 50 + 20 = 82). The measure of moral badness of that punch, as measured by painism, was 50 units of pain and not the Utilitarian's 82 units of pain.

By concentrating upon the maximum sufferer in each case the sheer numbers of individuals affected by an action becomes morally irrelevant. We are, instead, concerned with the maximum amount of suffering that is actually experienced. So, causing 5 units of pain to each of a thousand individuals is less wicked than causing, say, 1000 units of pain to one victim. This may be counterintuitive and, certainly, it goes against the conventional wisdom. Usually, for example, people take into account the numbers of victims of a war, but painism does not. We usually, but thoughtlessly, consider a war that causes a million casualties worse than a war that causes a thousand. But, according to painism, this is invalid. A war that causes intense agony to a thousand innocent people is worse than one that merely causes mild distress to a million. It is, according to painism, the intensity of individual suffering that matters and not the number of sufferers.

This, of course, has very serious consequences for the whole concept of democracy, as currently conceived, which is based upon the notion that the wishes of the majority take precedence over the wishes of the few. The assumption underlying democracy seems to be that wishes (votes) can be aggregated. (Wishes are precursors of pain-avoidance.) So painism, by rejecting aggregation, challenges the majoritarian problem of democracy. In other words painism proposes an alternative to democracy's 'tyranny of the majority'.

As regards the *trade-off problem* — painism accepts that such cost-benefit calculations are valid, provided they are balancing real *individual* experiences on both sides of the equation. So the individual pains relieved and caused, of the maximum sufferers, are what we take into account. Who benefited most from the punch to my jaw? Suppose my assailant's wife benefited because the punch reduced to zero the 20 units of pain she had been feeling because I had been obstinately sitting on her handbag. When I fell over, as a consequence of the punch, the handbag was retrieved. However, she then suffered anxiety about the fracas itself (perhaps 14 units of pain), so all that had been achieved by the punch in terms of her net benefits, amounted to a reduction in pain of 6 units. Let us say nobody else benefited. Thus, the cost of the punch was 50 units of pain to the *maximum sufferer* (the dog) and the net benefit to the *maximum beneficiary* (the wife) was only 6 units. So, was the punch justified? Clearly not!

In calculations of this sort there are always certain minor difficulties. The first, of course, is the *problem of the measurement* of pain and pain reduction. This has always been a difficulty, not just for painism, but for a number of other, more traditional, moral approaches. Today, however, the science of psychology can measure the strength of approach and avoidance behaviours and also, by using modern scanning techniques, objectively measure the intensity of activity in certain relevant areas of the brain. So this technical problem, although not yet solved, appears far less daunting than it did in the past.

The second minor difficulty also affects most moral systems and it concerns *motivation or intention*. Did the man who punched my jaw *intend* to break the dog's ribs? If he did not mean to do so then does this reduce the wickedness of the punch? According to painism, intention does not affect the issue (except when it comes to punishment). The broken ribs may not have been intended but they were still the consequence of the punch. Painism is not concerned with intentions, only with consequences. A virtue ethicist, of course, concerned mainly with the agent and not the victim, might argue that the man who threw the punch showed both valour and loyalty to his wife and so it was an act of virtue to have punched me. My toothache and the dog's ribs are ignored. I find such callousness unacceptable. Painism is concerned with *victims* and the *consequences* of actions rather than with the virtue or guilt of *agents*.

The third minor difficulty is the issue of *certainty*. How can we be sure, in advance, of the consequences of our actions? The answer is that we cannot. So when a scientist performs a painful experiment upon an animal in order to find a better treatment for toothache, is he justified? He is inflicting real pain in the here and now, merely in the hope of reducing others' toothache at some uncertain time in the future. He is seeking to trade-off *certain* pain against *hypothetical* benefit (Ryder 1998). When George Bush and Tony Blair attacked Iraq in 2003 they caused *predictable* death and suffering to thousands of innocent civilians and to hundreds of their own troops. They seem to have justified this by claiming that such actions would be out-weighed by *uncertain* benefits to many people in the future. Painism, however, is more concerned with the certain than with the uncertain; with the real than the unreal. Generally, the past is of less concern to painism than is the present because pains past are no longer actually experienced (except as painful memories). Later pains should matter more than earlier pains. With every individual it is important not that they *have lived* well but that they *will end* their lives happily. Dying is still a certainty for all of us and so the quality of dying is of supreme importance. It is morally better that someone lives indifferently but dies painlessly and without distress, than that they live well but die in agony.

We can aggregate pains and pleasures within the individual in the here and now but we cannot aggregate them over time. We cannot say, for example, that it does not matter that Miss Smith is dying in agony because, over the course of her life, if you add them all up, she has had so many pleasures. I am proposing that the end point practically trumps all that has gone before. But this does not mean that we should ignore the wellbeing of individuals during their lives and concentrate only upon ensuring that they have a good death; both matter, but the manner of dying is of particular moral importance to painism.

I have considered the detailed applications of painism elsewhere (Ryder 2001). One area that is obviously relevant is in the profession of medicine. Painism indicates that a far greater emphasis should be put by doctors upon the alleviation of suffering. Cures are, of course, supremely important but some diseases are bound to be terminal. In these cases, and in others, the need is for the skilled treatment of suffering in general, not only in the use of the best forms of analgesia but for the reduction of fear, anxiety and depression. Doctors and nurses should be trained to see their roles differently; not just as healers but as pain-reducers and happiness-makers also. Greater attention should be paid to the hospital environment. Wards are too often depressing and frightening places which more resemble workshops than havens of peace. Hospitals should learn from the luxury hotel trade how to provide a mentally uplifting environment. Hospices have led the way. But still the issue of euthanasia is cruelly avoided. Painism suggests that the offer of voluntary euthanasia to those suffering unstoppable pain, should be the final moral duty of a compassionate state.

If we accept that politics should be based upon morality and not exempted from moral theory as it often has been, then what would happen if political decisions were founded upon painism? Is a politician only to be concerned with the maximum sufferers? No, the maximum sufferer is both the measure of the badness of the situation and is the first person we should try to help if we can. But if we can help reduce the pains of several individuals simultaneously, in addition to the maximum sufferer's, then we should do so. If we are able only to help one individual at a time then we first help the maximum sufferer. If we cannot help the maximum sufferer but can only help lesser sufferers then, obviously, we should do so. If we succeed in reducing the overall suffering of the first maximum sufferer down to at least the level of suffering of the next highest sufferer then we switch our emphasis and try to help the latter also — and so on. If a terrorist bomb explodes killing ten people and wounding two dogs and twelve humans then the right thing to do is to try immediately to reduce the sufferings of *all* individuals and, only where priorities have to be made, to try to reduce the agonies of those suffering the most pain. If three humans and one of the dogs are writhing in pain then they should get the first shots of morphine. This does not mean that we should not also try to save the lives of others who are not in pain. One of the victims may be unconscious but bleeding to death: obviously it is important to stop her bleeding. We can then give analgesia and other care to those who are now the maximum sufferers — those with lesser wounds who have not yet had treatment. (The saving of life is important for several reasons and not least because death can cause great pain to relatives and friends.) Treatment over and above analgesia is also important and principally, according to painism, as a way of reducing future pains. A broken leg untreated will cause more pain in the future than one that is properly treated right away. But, according to painism, the reduction of individual suffering, present and future, is always the central objective. Such an approach is different from traditional triage where treatability rather than the intensity of suffering takes priority.

Clearly, it is not only the *causing* of pain that is wrong it is also wrong not to try to reduce the pains of others with whom we are *not* directly connected. Neglecting others' pain is as bad as causing it and 'passing by on the other side of the road' is wrong. We all should be involved in our day to day lives in doing what we can reasonably do to help others, and this applies to governments too. Living in a secluded monastery, doing no harm, is not enough; we should engage with the world and attempt to reduce suffering wherever we can. Of course, it is unreasonable to expect everyone to be a saint; so we must be able to get on with our lives as teachers, builders, fathers and mothers but, when we encounter suffering that is unattended, we should do what we reasonably can to reduce it. Politicians are in a powerful position to do this by becoming involved in national and international campaigns to reduce suffering (whether caused by infringements of liberty, justice, equality, democracy or by any other cause) and it is absolutely right that they do so. Sometimes they are criticised if this entails neglecting suffering on their doorstep. Charity, so it is said, begins at home; yet this cliché can become a pretext for inaction, laziness and indifference. With the internet, television and radio, the world is now our doorstep. In judging who are the maximum sufferers politicians must, today, cast their eyes around the whole globe and take into account the sufferings of all races, religions and species.

If politicians were to use painism as the moral basis for their policies, this would have different results from applying Utilitarianism. Utilitarianism has had a distinguished history in achieving many of the social, economic, legal and political reforms of the nineteenth century, although critics have rightly argued that the principles of justice and liberty demand also the protection of basic rights (to life, liberty, freedom of expression etc.), irrespective of Utilitarian calculations. Utilitarianism, however, is blind when it comes to the *distribution* of happiness (or pain-reduction): a thousand people enjoying mild satisfaction might justify the agony of one, or the ecstasy of a small elite might excuse the boredom of the many. Painism does not accept such a situation. It sides automatically with the individuals in pain. Painism, here, seems to resemble Rights Theory; it safeguards the individual and protects the citizen from the over-mighty state. Does painism, then, amount to the same thing as Rights Theory? In particular cases it may have the same effect but painism is analogue rather than digital: it is a sliding scale whereas Rights are discrete and defined. Rights Theory provides neat rules of thumb but, like all rules, they can be clumsy and psychologically insensitive. Mr Smith, for example, may suffer intensely if deprived of his right to freedom of speech but Mr Jones could not care less. Painism is sensitive to such individual differences; according to painism it is worth campaigning for Mr Smith's freedom of speech but not so much for Mr Jones'. Furthermore, painism sees under the surface of rights such as the rights to liberty, equality and justice because such rights only matter when they contribute to our happiness and pain-reduction. Painism, in this sense, is more profound and more accurate than Rights Theory.

The Iraq War

The decision to attack Iraq in 2003 was the epitome of what is wrong with modern Western democracy. It was a decision based neither upon facts nor morality. In retrospect we can now see that the war was a moral turning point in politics and it provides a clear paradigm that is worth examining in detail. It was an example of a war that was both immoral and, probably, illegal. Tony Blair, otherwise almost certainly to be judged a very good Prime Minister, made this one monumental error.

Almost unbelievably, Britain went to war five times in the six years 1997–2003 but on most occasions most people were satisfied that Britain was fighting on the side of right. But in the case of the Iraq war of 2003 there was much disquiet. On 5 March 2004 Tony Blair sought to justify the war in a speech in his constituency of Sedgefield. Much of this speech was political argument about the risks posed by terrorism if combined with modern weaponry, and he made justified criticisms of the efficiency and outdated constitution of the United Nations. At the ethical level, however, it was disappointing. Blair blurred a good argument (the case for humanitarian intervention) with a bad argument (the alleged threat of Iraq's weapons of mass destruction) and concluded from this that pre-emptive war was justified both in this case and generally. Two years earlier, on 2 March 2003, Blair had tried to give a coherent moral justification for the war he was about to start (The Prime Minister Answers, *Independent*, 2 March 2003): 'I would never go into a war if I thought it were morally wrong or if I thought it was not in the best interests of this country', he wrote. He compared the Iraq situation with his military interventions in Kosovo and Afghanistan, unaware, apparently, of the significant moral differences — 'both led to innocent people being killed … (but) we did the right thing.' When asked by Judy Moore of Norwich whether he was concerned that such a war would expose Britain to greater threat from Islamic-based terrorism, Blair replied 'one of the main reasons Saddam must not be allowed to retain his weapons of mass destruction is to reduce this threat'. Moore commented: 'I wonder what Tony Blair knows that the rest of us don't. He seems to be courting disaster from a place of utter conviction — but I don't quite understand where that conviction is coming from.' Blair, it has been alleged, would often make decisions before he had seen supporting evidence and without Cabinet discussion, acting 'presidentially'.

On 18 March 2003 Blair, on the eve of battle, likened the situation to that in 1939, as Britain faced the threat from Nazi Germany. Again, he seemed unaware of the historical and moral differences. Hitler, by 1939, had already, over the course of some years, demonstrated not only his ruthlessness and anti-semitism but his military expansionism through massive re-armament, remilitarising the Rhineland, annexing Sudetenland, absorbing Austria, destroying Czechoslovakia and, finally, invading Poland. The analogy with Saddam was, at the very least, somewhat shaky. London was well over two thousand miles from Baghdad but barely two hundred from Germany, and well within range of German aircraft. By using this false analogy Blair seemed to imply a similarity between himself and Winston Churchill. The senses of exaggerated threat and messianic self-importance are clearly evident. A few weeks later on British television, President Bush (driven by the morally-bankrupt policies of his Vice President and Donald Rumsfeld) sought to justify the Iraq war in vague terms of 'security' and 'justice' (BBC 1 News, 6 April 2003). At home, Bush had already described liberty for the Iraqi people as 'God's gift to every human being in the world' (Singer 2004, p 208). As Peter Singer commented — 'many American Christians see their own nation as carrying out a divine mission'. Bush's references to 'the evil ones' and 'the axis of evil' clearly appealed to this constituency. Both Bush and Blair consider themselves to be devoutly Christian yet their policy on the Iraq war was manifestly unChristian. Singer points out that although Bush seems to use a Utilitarian argument to justify the Iraq war he inconsistently rejects such an approach to other issues such as stem cell research:

> If he is prepared to argue in Utilitarian terms that a war that kills innocents is justified because it saves many more innocents from being murdered under Saddam, he should be prepared to accept the same calculus of costs and benefits for using a few embryos to save many more lives (Singer 2004, p 170).

Traditionally, recourse to war has been excused on some half a dozen grounds—proportionality, right intention, last resort, legitimate authority, prospects of success and just cause. In the case of the Iraq war just about all of these grounds (except, at the time, prospects of success) were dubious. Was the war in proportion to the evil it strove to put right? (Saddam was removed but many were killed and thousands of children and other civilians were injured and permanently handicapped in the process. After the initial war there were chaos, hardship and suicide bombings.) Was there right intention? (Or were there, as seems likely, hidden motives such as oil?) Was it a last resort? (No, UN sanctions and weapon inspections could have been continued.) Was there legitimate authority? (The United Nations, the pope, many individual states and other organisations were essentially opposed to the war. Were, then, Blair and Bush legitimate authorities? Maybe, but large numbers of their own citizens were against them.)

Most important of all these 'post-Christian' traditional criteria is the argument of *just cause*. Basically, wars have been justified either on the grounds of self-defence or of rescuing another state from outside attack. Did either of these justifications apply in the case of Iraq in 2003? No evidence of weapons of mass destruction or of terroristic links that seriously threatened the West were found. (The terrorist link argument was one of the most implausible. For years Saddam had been a stern opponent of most Islamic terrorist groups.) There are, certainly, good reasons for seeking to contain terrorism, yet President Bush made little apparent effort before invading either Afghanistan or Iraq to control terrorism by trying to understand and reduce its causes—the most blatant of which was Israel's chronic oppression of the Palestinians. Was there, then, evidence that Iraq was being attacked and that the Coalition was going in to protect them? No. The ground emphasised by Tony Blair at the time was that the West was threatened by Iraqi weapons of mass destruction (WMD). Then how about other states with WMD such as North Korea, Israel, France and India—should these have been invaded also? President Bush, on the other hand, argued that an additional reason for war was 'regime change'. This was both more persuasive and more honest than Blair, although he did not make it clear why regime change was deemed to be necessary in this case rather than in a score of other dictatorships as well. Would such a change be solely for the benefit of the Iraqis themselves or would there be some advantage in it for the US — safer oil supplies, for example? Blair may have privately believed that regime change was the main objective but he rarely said so publicly before the war, either because he knew that the UN could not accept this as a legal cause, or because he believed the British public would not see this reason as a justification for war. If so, he was probably mistaken in the latter case as, ironically, this excuse might have been far more acceptable than the one he selected. All in all, Bush and Blair were seen by some as rather casual in their attitude to war, ordering it as just a standard form of foreign policy enforcement. They seemed to lack the dread of war that was a characteristic of the older generation of statesmen who had been alive in World War II and of some military people who have actually experienced war. Indeed, some thought that they appeared to relish it. In the event, the Iraq war of 2003–2004 killed hundreds of young Western soldiers, at least twenty thousand innocent Iraqis and wounded tens of thousands of others. (If numbers matter.) Killings and woundings continued for years. The war was an unprovoked attack leading, as war inevitably does, to the agony and death of many innocent people. It has been said that there had been no such unprovoked war caused by Western powers since Hitler invaded Poland in 1939, and that Britain has not waged such an unprovoked war for well over a hundred years.

Unlike Hitler (who had his own warped ethical code), Blair and Bush were professed Christians. Yet there appears little in Christian ethics to justify their actions in this case. To the contrary, what they did has seemed to several Christian religious leaders to be entirely antithetical to Christianity and to Jesus' teachings of peace, love and the turning of the other cheek. So, how is this to be explained? Perhaps the two men shared some special sense of mission or a special interpretation of Christian ethics? As already stated (p. 63), paranoid fantasies typically include an exaggerated fear of attack (in the absence of real evidence), together with the religiose sense of being a saviour (the messianic complex). Indeed, these are the two principal characteristics of paranoid disorders. Such thought patterns are common enough among the mentally disturbed.

According to reports in *The Independent* newspaper (7 October 2005) President Bush told Palestinian leaders:

> I'm driven with a mission from God. God would tell me, 'George, go and fight those terrorists in Afghanistan.' And I did, and then God would tell me, 'George, go and end the tyranny in Iraq,' and I did.

If this is accurate, then it is suggestive of paranoid delusional thinking. Bush might even be describing auditory hallucinations—a classic sign of mental illness. Taken together with a few lesser indications such as Bush's strangely inappropriate smile which flickered across his face when he was talking of war (inappropriate affect being sometimes a sign of serious disorder), then this could have been a disturbing picture of a man who might possibly need psychiatric treatment rather than being left in charge of the world's greatest nuclear arsenal. (There seems no obvious mechanism for getting rid of Presidents or Prime Ministers who are insane or paranoid.) Paranoia and paranoid personality disorder are not the same as paranoid schizophrenia; serious abnormality of thought can occur in the absence of schizophrenic or other illness. A well-known feature of some paranoid disorders is where two individuals encourage each other's fantasies in a so-called *folie à deux,* rather as may have occurred in the Bush–Blair relationship. However well disguised and concealed—as paranoid conditions typically are—such thinking, although claiming to be principled, is rarely supported by rational and convincing ethical argument. To be fair to Blair, however, he did seem to be a man concerned about moral principle, and perhaps he acted on a principled and rational moral position on this occasion. If so, what could this have been? He has not yet explained. Let us briefly review two other possibilities.

We have already considered and discarded both the Christian and the traditional post-Christian justifications (the 'just war' position). They simply do not justify the Iraq war of 2003. Would the war, then, be justifiable in Kantian terms? A Kantian view of ethics includes a respect for law and a requirement to act on principle rather than pragmatism. Most importantly, Kant argued that we should treat humanity never as a means but always also as an end. This implies a strong and principled respect for individual persons. Was this apparent in the Coalition's killing and wounding of thousands of Iraqi civilians? It is hard to see that it was.

We seem, then, to be left only with a Utilitarian defence of the war —the argument that the war's aggregated benefits (in terms of happiness) outweighed its aggregated pains. If we add up each person's (largely unknown) benefits from being freed from Saddam's tyranny and then add up all the (actual) pains of the people wounded, bereaved, terrified and rendered homeless or jobless in the war and its bloody aftermath (including the increase of terrorism in Europe) then the balance, at best, is unclear. In the very long term, perhaps, the total of benefits may one day be claimed to outweigh all the pains (although I personally reject the validity of such Utilitarian 'aggregations' of pains and pleasures, see p. 74). Some of the world's leading Utilitarian philosophers, however, such as Peter Singer, opposed the war. Nevertheless, as we have seen, some sort of vague Utilitarian thinking seemed to underlie official policy. It was an argument that Blair, for example, seemed to use on television on at least one occasion; in early 2003, he sought to justify the war by saying that the innocent victims of his war would be 'far fewer' than the victims of Saddam's wars. Yet two years after the invasion it seemed that more Iraqis were being killed and tortured than in Saddam's reign.

Let us assume for a moment that Utilitarianism is sound. The Utilitarian position could have been put like this: 'We are attacking your country in order to free your ordinary citizens from the oppression of a cruel dictator.' To some extent, George Bush did actually say this but Tony Blair gave this reason only a subordinate status at the time. Yet such regime change (or 'humanitarian intervention') is, surely, a good argument. As we have seen, old ideas about the so-called immunity of heads of state have taken a knock since the arrest of General Pinochet in Britain in1998. Heads of state and prime ministers are nowadays, and quite rightly, regarded as especially culpable for state crimes committed against their own as well as other peoples. This is a major step in the right direction. Dictators should now beware. If they resort to gross injustices, wars, oppressions or tortures of their own peoples or of others, then they risk being targeted by the international community and eventually brought to trial. The boundaries of a nation no longer give protection from international law and ethics. Maybe the Israeli practice of targeting the cars of leading terrorists will catch on internationally and wicked dictators will be taken out by precise UN approved missile attacks. At any rate, the old boys' club among politicians seems to be on the way out. Instead of preserving the safety of political and military leaders regardless of their behaviour (the 'we VIPs must all stick together' approach) such influential people are now being called to account by bodies such as the United Nations and the International Criminal Court (ICC) at the Hague; indictment, or 'naming and shaming', are increasingly being used as a sanction, and quite rightly. Western leaders, too, are susceptible to arrest. Oddly, the ICC does not have jurisdiction covering the offence of waging illegal war, and the UK courts require the authority of the Attorney General before a Prime Minister can be so charged. Once out of office, however, an ex-leader lacks this protection (Sands 2003, 2005).

If the war in Iraq in 2003 was solely to do with regime change, then surely this could have been done by the capture or killing of Saddam Hussein by special forces. It appears that this was actually tried but found to be impossible. Why, then, were Western politicians so reluctant to talk about this failure publicly? The answer may be that they feared that public opinion would not yet accept such tactics. It might be a step forward if international law and the UN Charter could be amended so that the UN could authorise the arrest or, if resisted, even the killing of egregious dictators.

In early 2004 polls indicated that half the population of the UK thought the war unjustified and mainly, so it seemed, because of the huge burden of suffering and death it imposed upon already oppressed civilians. On the other hand, the reason most given by those who favoured the war was not the safeguarding of oil, the removal of weapons of mass destruction, nor the suppression of international terrorism, but the deposing of a cruel dictator. But the moral dilemma remained — is it right to kill and maim innocent civilians in order to save them from a dictatorship? How can one protect their rights by thus infringing them? Killing and maiming are the far more *certain* results of war than is freedom from any form of tyranny. We can recall that the NATO bombing of Serb aggressors in Kosovo and Bosnia in 1999 met with widespread public approval. Why did this receive so much more approval than the Coalition bombing of Baghdad in 2003? Some differences were that the cruelty of the Serbs towards Muslim civilians was extreme, worsening and on Western television screens while Saddam's cruelty was chronic, insidious and partly concealed. In the Iraq war, television had to rely upon pictures of Kurdish victims gassed fifteen years earlier at a time when Saddam was supported by the West. Furthermore, it is uncertain that such deaths were crueller than those of civilians killed by Coalition conventional bombing. (Some gases — as used by the Russians, for example, in the Chechen Moscow Siege of 2002 — can be relatively humane if used correctly.) In the case of Kosovo, there was not massive bombing of civilian targets by the West, nor was the aggressor seen to be an individual dictator (Saddam) but a people (the Serbs). Guilt was thus perceived to be widespread and so the deaths of Serbs, although regretted, was judged to be more morally acceptable. Blair's military intervention in Kosovo was thus approved — it was seen in Britain as a rescue operation launched to save innocent Moslem victims from unjust and outrageous Serbian aggression.

As we have seen, the version of the 'just war' theory that is traditionally encapsulated in international law is that the only justification for going to war is as a defence against aggression (Norman 1995). This takes the form either of self-defence or the defence of others. Intervening to protect weaker children from the school bully or to rescue the victim of a street mugging are generally accepted as good things to do. But can this defence be used to justify regime change? Can 'oppression' be a substitute for the word 'aggression'? I think it can, because both cause pain.

Much of this argument assumes that the Utilitarian position is valid although I have argued (Ryder 2001) that adding up the pleasures and sufferings of separate individuals produces no meaningful score. One cannot say that causing the deaths of a thousand people in war is worse than causing the deaths of a hundred, nor that causing agony to a million is worse than causing agony to a thousand. Each individual can only die once and can only suffer their own suffering. Nobody can directly suffer the agonies of others. Such Utilitarian misconceptions are common; it is routinely assumed, for example, that disasters causing many casualties are worse than those causing a few, that mass murders are worse than single killings, and that the wickedness of wars can be measured by the *numbers of casualties*. According to painism, however, the pain of each individual matters absolutely. Nations, of course, feel no pain themselves. Indeed, the wickedness of an event, according to painism, can be measured not by the number of its victims but by the intensity of the suffering of the individual who suffers most. So, causing agony to one person is worse than causing mild pain to many. This is, as already explained, a central tenet of the theory of *painism*. Pain (by which is meant any sort of suffering) is an *experience* and unless it is actually experienced then it is not real pain. The justification of the Iraq war on the grounds that 'only a few thousand suffered and died' is thus, according to painism, totally invalid. Essentially, if regime change or humanitarian intervention was the justification for the war then the whole operation was similar to a

police operation to arrest a sadistic murderer, a school bully or a sus-
pected terrorist. But if any police force in the civilised world, in the
pursuit of such laudable aims, kill, abuse and wound innocent men,
women and children in the process, then they are strongly criticised.
People will say their action was not morally justified, it was not professional, it was not worth it and it was out of all proportion. The
same should apply to armies. By all means, particularly if the United
Nations agrees, remove the cruel dictators in this world, but do so
only if you can do it without causing mayhem. We know that the
so-called smart bombing of Baghdad caused agonising injuries to
Iraqi children and maimed some of them for life (Warren 2004). The
bombs were simply not smart enough. Today, children are para-
lysed and limbless because of the war we waged. Some will go on
suffering for years. Can the eventual arrest of a dishevelled dictator
in a hole in the ground ever justify such cruelty? Are innocent little
children of less moral importance than a dictator? (Ryder 2004)

Ways Forward

Lessons can be drawn from the experience of the Iraq war, and various attempts to improve democracy have been proposed. Could it be
more direct or participatory, for example, involving the electorate in
frequent referendums and consultations? Apathy might become a
problem in such a system, leading to non-involvement, so it has been
suggested that it should be made an offence for voters not to vote.
Would this be right? Participating in government brings pleasure to
many and this is a worthwhile asset of democracy, but such participation does not bring pleasure to all. People differ in their tastes and
interests. Particularly during periods of good governance, when
most people feel relatively satisfied, some voters tend not to feel the
need to participate at all. Democracy can, in this sense, become a victim of its own success.

The basic international acceptance of democracy (tempered by
civil rights) remains high and in the last thirty years we have seen its
principles and practices extended to the work place and to the home.
Difficulties, however, remain. Minorities still have to decide, for
example, whether or not to support majority decisions with which
they disagree. I might be convinced that the right policy morally is X
while the elected government (allegedly representing the majority)
chooses to do Y. Should my belief in the moral importance of democracy itself mean that I should support and help to enforce Y even
though I believe it is morally wrong? This is rather like a board of

directors, of which I am a member, taking a decision that I disagree with; am I bound by 'corporate responsibility' to pay lip service to the policy I detest? Should I show 'loyalty' to my country (or the company) even if I believe they are morally wrong? Which moral principle takes precedence? Loyalty or truth? I can resign from a board but not from my country. These are old problems and they remain. Painism may help to resolve them by looking under the surface at what really matters — the suffering of the greatest sufferers. We should remember that most traditional slogans such as liberty, equality, justice and democracy are just secondary manifestations of what really counts morally: the happiness of others.

In as much as groups of people rarely agree unanimously, democracy may be a good procedure for making decisions. We vote and those in the majority determine the way we decide to go. Yet more effort could be made by democratic institutions to assess whether such majority decisions will actually have the consequences desired by the majority. Opinions may differ for several reasons. People may all be wanting the same *goal* but differ in their opinions as to the most effective *means* of achieving it. This is a matter for science. If everyone wants less inflation, say, but differ as to how to achieve this, then it should be possible to resolve the dispute by ascertaining the correct answer empirically. More profound grounds for disagreement occur when the minority wants a different *goal* from the majority. Usually, both minority and majority are voting for their own interests. But sometimes people vote altruistically, for the 'greater good' or for some other interest.

There is a contemporary preference for open and free discussion. The willingness of democratic governments to listen, consult, publish their deliberations and, indeed, publicly to investigate their failures, are healthy features of modern democracies. Persuasion rather than coercion is the order of the day. Such 'public reasonableness' also encourages the virtue of compromise — often a necessary eventuality in complex and pluralistic societies. *Compromise, moderation and a dislike of fanaticism* are well established and prized features of the British (and especially the English) culture and are essential to democracy; the principle that no no principles are absolute. Some other cultures lack this high evaluation of compromise, seeing issues in stark terms of right or wrong, and viewing compromise as weakness. Such cultures may find democracy difficult.

The situation in Northern Ireland has been an example of this, with two conflicting sectarian sub-cultures, neither of which traditionally has respected compromise or toleration, being constantly at loggerheads. A process of debate and consultation in modern democracies now precedes decisions and strives for consensus. Those who are eventually outvoted can, at least, expect to know the reasons for the vote going against them. They can also feel that they have had their say. Politicians in a democracy establish a subculture which expects them to be able to 'agree to disagree' and to remain on terms with those who have outvoted them. This is the *deliberative democracy* that we find in many modern states today. Yet it appears to coincide with a growing apathy towards politics in general. Only on special issues in Britain, such as the Iraq war of 2003, where public emotions were fully aroused, have we recently seen spontaneous massed political demonstrations. In Britain, the protection of the countryside, the disillusionment with globalization and opposition to the export of live animals have been other, lesser, examples of political enthusiasm and participation in politics at street level. Little has been seriously suggested as to how participation or 'good citizenship', can be encouraged or enforced. Kymlicka asks why there are not more 'good Samaritan' laws to promote participation and other forms of good citizenship, or mandatory voting or mandatory public service (Kymlicka 2002, p 316).

As the stoical denial of pain becomes less of a cultural feature, people appear to be increasingly sensitive to the sufferings of others and committed to remedial action. The time seems ripe, therefore, for a more painist approach to politics. What, in general terms, would this mean? First, it would mean an end to the *numbers game* whereby public policy and moral judgements are influenced largely by the number of human individuals affected by any action. For instance, if one policy benefits 5% of the population and an alternative policy benefits 50% then the latter, today, is automatically adopted. Painism challenges this by insisting that *it is the degree of individual pain and pain-reduction that matters, and not the number of sufferers.* This change in outlook would radically affect economic and social policies as well as attitudes to war and the environment. A concern for the well-being of each individual is paramount under painism.

Secondly, painism removes the rigidity of applying Rights criteria and provides a *more realistic and flexible* approach. Rights are seen as secondary considerations. They are important only in that they frequently happen to reduce and avoid pain (suffering). But individuals differ widely in their needs and tastes. To insist that everyone has

to join a trade union, have privacy and enjoy a right to religious freedom, for example, and that these should be universal elements in *all*
policy, overlooks the fact that for many people trade unions, privacy
or religion are of little or no concern. A list of rights is merely a useful
approximation of what makes individuals happy. It is not precise.
Why, therefore, distort policies in this way? Denying one person the
right to join a union may cause them 100 units of pain but may cause
another person only 2 units of pain or no pain at all. Applying Rights
Theory across the board seems unnecessarily clumsy. One man's
meat is another's poison. What we should be concerned about is the
happiness of individuals. Applying rights may be a rough and ready
rule of thumb for doing this, but painism would be a far more accurate approach. It might require more detailed research into the consequences of policies on individuals but that, in principle, could be
done. Indeed, to base public policy upon scientific findings would be
a considerable step forward.

Thirdly, basing public policy on painism would not only
emphasise the *importance of individuals*, it would also *focus attention
upon suffering*. Certain areas such as health and health promotion
would thus tend to gain in significance. Areas where the state traditionally has caused suffering would also come under scrutiny —
policing, prisons, the justice system generally, defence and war,
would all need to be examined. Our prisons are full of mentally ill
people; is this right? Where individuals are not caused pain there
would be no need for laws prohibiting certain behaviours; for example, laws against consenting sex could be dispensed with. It is
extraordinary that there are still laws on the book that can send a 35
year old woman to prison for allowing herself to be carried upstairs
by a 14 year old boy and being made love to (Daily Mail, 27 September 2000, p 5). How cruel that both these innocent individuals should
be forced to undergo a police enquiry and trial, and that the woman
should be sent to jail and hounded by the press. The law, based upon
some outdated pastiche of morality, is indeed an ass in this case, as it
is in many others. Painism could sweep away wicked nanny state
restrictions of this sort and discourage the modern puritanical cam-
paign against various harmless pleasures. The processes of 'criminal
justice' are themselves sometimes unjust and criminal. Trials are
made unnecessarily cruel by the routine public naming of defendants, for example, and by a system that is adversarial rather than a
search for truth. It should be an offence to publish the names of
defendants before conviction; everyone, supposedly, is innocent

until proved guilty. Holding captive uncharged individuals for weeks, pending laborious police investigations, whether on remand or under suspicion of terrorism, causes suffering and is also wrong. (The moral grounds for custody before conviction are highly dubious.)

Fourthly, the tension between the underlying Utilitarianism of much of our legislation and those human rights that are invoked to moderate this, could be avoided. Painism and its preeminent concern with maximum sufferers undercuts both Utilitarian and rights approaches and provides *a unified moral system*.

Fifthly, *the problem of conflicting rights*, as often found in the application of Rights Theory, could be avoided. There would be no need to argue over which right takes precedence. The question would simply be which action causes the least suffering to individuals, and the greater happiness. Such issues are now open to scientific assessment.

Finally, the suffering of *all* individuals, regardless as to class, race, religion, age or species, could be given equal consideration. For the first time, governments would be required to adopt fair and equal policies for nonhuman as well as human individuals, and adopting a Rights approach for the rich but a Utilitarian approach for the poor, for example, would no longer be tolerated.

So, in general, one can tentatively propose painism as being a possible advance for politics generally and for political decision-making. The downside is that a great deal more psychological research into the needs and desires of individuals would have to be undertaken. Instead of government's usual blunderbuss approach to legislation, a far more piecemeal procedure would have to be developed; one sensitive to the different desires and pains of individuals. One department of government should be charged with the job of constantly searching for and helping, on an individual basis, the greatest sufferers; another should ensure that all policy decisions are made upon good scientific grounds and that these are published. Consider, for example, the use of speed cameras: thousands of motorists every year are fined or deprived of their licences because they exceed an arbitrary speed limit. Nobody knows (because no government scientist collects this evidence) how many die each year when they brake suddenly on seeing a camera, or because they are looking for police cars rather than at the road ahead, or because they commit suicide when, without a licence, they lose their jobs. This nasty piece of lucrative domestic tyranny is not based upon proper even-handed and unselective science at all. It should be. Much government so-called science is at a similarly primitive level.

Just as local councils seem to proliferate unnecessary traffic regulations to justify their existence, so national governments churn out oppressive and unnecessary laws, some of them worryingly restrictive of civil liberties; authority to tap telephones, to introduce ID cards, to use security body scanners, to monitor websites and to establish DNA databases. Big Brother is already here! There needs to be a charter to protect individuals, and repeal the scores of laws that already exist. The arrogance of government is measured by the number of laws passed and wars waged. Why should state-controlled violence against civilians, whether by police or military, be any more morally acceptable than the violence of a terrorist? Other things being equal, violence or oppression by the state is even less morally acceptable than violence or oppression by individuals.

Overall, painism as the moral basis for politics, although not the only way, would encourage two things that modern educated and rational societies surely deserve: public policies based upon scientifically established facts and on a clearly argued moral theory. Painism's emphasis upon *the intensity of suffering* rather than the *quantity of sufferers*, and its dispensing with the necessity for artificial rules (such as are required by rights legislation) means that laws could be tailor-made for specific situations, and for individuals and minorities with special needs. Licences could more often be issued to allow exemptions from general laws. Levels of suffering could be measured by social and psychological research and from the scientific observation of human approach and avoidance behaviours, including measures of the levels of 'penalties' that individuals are prepared to pay in order to avoid certain situations. Preferences, too, could be established. Objective measures are already used by animal welfare scientists in measuring the intensity of preferences in non-human animals, and similar techniques could be applied in the human case (Ryder 1975, 1989, 1998; Radford 2001; Broom & Johnson 1993; Webster 1994). Humans are animals too. Physiological measures of stress are already in use and the development of increasingly direct and non-intrusive measures of brain indices of suffering and pleasure can be anticipated in future years. Government policies and legislation in the future should become vastly more refined, more precise in enforcing Mill's ubiquitous harm principle and generally more direct in responding to what really matters — *suffering* itself (Ryder 2001).

Conclusions

We have ranged over the field of political philosophy from the days of Plato and extracted many moral principles upon which politics can be based. We have also looked at several of the modern issues underlying politics to see how they connect with ethical foundations.

As we have seen, the case of war highlights the need for stating the moral objects that underlie policy (pp. 80–87). The justification for pre-emptive war is a difficult and dangerous doctrine, and the Iraq war exemplified this; it is too easy for powerful nations to invade others on the grounds that they *may* pose some vague threat, just as it is too easy for police to shoot unarmed foreigners on the grounds that they *may* be suicide bombers, or to lock them up on similar grounds. It seems that the Coalition went to war with Saddam Hussein not only without properly *ascertaining the facts* as regards weapons of mass destruction, *but also without a clear moral theory*. Is it too much to ask of governments, that before committing to wars in future, they should be absolutely clear both as regards facts and morality?

Governments seem prone to be motivated by mere whim and sentiment. Many of their policies appear to be undisciplined either by science or philosophy and, as we have found, no coherent moral statement was publicly uttered by government in the approach to the Iraq war of 2003. When interviewed by the media, war leaders merely mouthed a few moral slogans, snatches of post-Christian dogma jumbled with Utilitarianism. Such gobbledygook would not have passed an ethics exam for ten year olds (Ryder 2004)!

As we have seen, it is impossible to justify the Iraq 2003 war on Christian, traditional, Kantian or painist grounds (see pp. 80–85). Only an optimistic application of Utilitarian principles might suffice. Yet even leading Utilitarians were opposed to this war. If we can conclude anything, it is this: in Western democracies thousands of electors now require more of their political leaders. We need them to explain their policies rationally, giving to us not only the scientific facts, but also a coherent moral argument. The application of painism to politics is only one way to do this. There are several other rational moral theories. Like some of these, painism is consistent with a part of our nature: that part which manifests as our natural impulse of compassion. The moral theory of painism is a rationalised scheme that rides upon the back of this natural 'hard-wired' compassion and takes advantage of its motive power (see pp. 42–43, 56, 73). The protective urge may be strongest towards our offspring and our mates but it can be extended way beyond our family and our tribe to include those of other races and species. With the remarkable reasoning power of the human brain, we can systematise and make firm this tendency. The range of compassion grows wider as our understanding widens to recognise and include all painient things within our moral circle. The implication of painism is that *political policies should extend to individuals of all nations, races and species on an 'equal pain equal treatment' basis*. Realistically speaking, this will not happen immediately, but I hope that it will eventually. We should, therefore, reinforce and nurture our impulses of love, compassion and protectiveness and even our innate horrors of blood and injury. These are all valuable instincts that help us to control aggression and contain our hurtful impulses. Modern warfare's use of long range weapons and distant chains of command mean that these natural defences against war and destruction are not triggered as once they were in hand to hand conflict. So we have to be especially careful. Wars, to be legitimate, should be entirely under a reformed UN control. The UN charter needs to be amended to allow the use of controlled and focused force to neutralise dictators on humanitarian (or painist) grounds. Weapons should be developed that are restraining and tranquillising in their effects, so that authorised arrests can be made humanely without the spilling of blood or the causing of pain. Weapons also need to be far 'smarter' so that only specified offenders (e.g. dictators) are affected by them, and not thousands of innocent bystanders.

War highlights the deficiencies in modern politics. All policies, however, need to address the question: 'What moral theory does this policy aim to satisfy?' A range of rational moral theories are available. Personally, I favour the approach that I call painism; a theory based upon the premise that the boundaries of painience are the edges of the individual (pp. 73–80). The application of painism would concentrate the politicians' minds on the happiness of each individual affected by the policy, rather than upon the size of the majorities in favour. Whatever the difficulties, I hope the case has been made for putting morality back into politics. Although no moral theory may be held to be entirely convincing, there is, surely, still the need for open and competent moral debate during the formulation of policy. Policies should be founded not upon irrational notions, nor upon mere expediency, but only upon facts and careful moral argument.

Ethics, as a rational enterprise, will often conflict with other, more negative, aspects of our natures and help to curb our natural impulses to conquer, compete and kill. By putting morality back into politics and basing our policies upon our compassion and upon the sufferings of all individuals, regardless of their superficial differences, we should be able to build a happier future.

References

Argyle, Michael (1987): *The Psychology of Happiness*, Methuen

Axelrod, Robert (1984): *The Evolution of Cooperation*, Basic Books

Beitz, Charles (1979): *Political Theory and International Relations*, Princeton University Press

Benewick, Robert and Green, Philip eds (1992): *The Routledge Dictionary of Twentieth Century Political Thinkers*, Routledge

Bentham, Jeremy (1780): *Introduction to the Principles of Morals and Legislation*, Chapter 17

Broom, D M and K G Johnson (1993): *Stress in Animal Welfare*, Chapman & Hall

Brown, Alan (1986): *Modern Political Philosophy: Theories of the Just Society*, Penguin Books

Brown, Chris (1993): 'International Affairs' in *A Companion to Contemporary Political Philosophy*, ed Robert E Goodin and Philip Pettit, Blackwell

Dawkins, Richard (1976): *The Selfish Gene*, Oxford University Press

Dower, Nigel and Williams, John eds (2002): *Global Citizenship: A Critical Reader*, Edinburgh University Press

Dunne, Tim and Nicholas Wheeler, ed (1999): *Human Rights in Global Politics*, Cambridge University Press

Galston, William (1991): *Liberal Purposes : Goods, Virtues, and Duties in the Liberal State*, Cambridge University Press

Garner, Robert (1988): *Political Animals : Animal Protection Politics in Britain and the United States*, Macmillan Press

Garner, Robert (1993): *Animals, Politics and Morality*, Manchester University Press

Giddens, Anthony (1998): *The Third Way : The Renewal of Social Democracy*, Polity Press

Giddens, Anthony (2000): *The Third Way and Its Critics*, Polity Press

Glover, Jonathan (1977): *Causing Death and Saving Lives*, Penguin Books

Goodin, Robert E and Pettit, Philip eds (1993): *A Companion to Contemporary Political Philosophy*, Blackwell

Gray, John (2002): *Straw Dogs: Thoughts on Humans and Other Animals*, Granta Publications

HMSO (1995): *Human Rights*, HMSO

Hampton, Jean (1995): 'Contract and Consent' *in A Companion to Contemporary Political Philosophy*, ed Robert E. Goodin & Philip Pettit, Blackwell

Heywood, Andrew (2000): *Key Concepts in Politics*, MacMillan Press

Ignatieff, Peter (2001): *Human Rights as Politics and Idolatry*, Princeton University Press

Independent, 'The Prime Minister Answers', 2nd March 2003

Knowles, Dudley (2001): *Political Philosophy*, Routledge

Kymlicka, Will (1993): 'Community' in *A Companion to Contemporary Political Philosophy*, ed Robert E Goodin and Philip Pettit, Blackwell

Kymlicka, Will (2002): *Contemporary Political Philosophy : An Introduction*, 2nd Edition,   Oxford University Press

Leopold, Aldo (1949): *Sand County Almanac*

Lessnoff, Michael H (1999): *Political Philosophers of the Twentieth Century*, Blackwell

Lincoln, Abraham (1864): *Gettysburg Address*

Mansbridge, Jane and Susan Moller Okin (1993): 'Feminism' in *A Companion to Contemporary Political Philosophy*, ed Robert E Goodin and Philip Pettit, Blackwell

Martin, Paul (2005): *Making Happy People*, Fourth Estate

Mill, John Stuart (1859): *On Liberty*. Modern edition *John Stuart Mill on Liberty and Other Essays*, ed John Gray, Oxford University Press, 1991

Mill, John Stuart (1863): *Utilitarianism*

Miller, David (2003): *Political Philosophy*, Open University Press

Nettle, Daniel (2004): *Happiness*, Open University Press

Norman, Richard (1995): *Ethics and Killing in War*, Cambridge University Press

Pinker, Steven (1997): *How the Mind Works*, W.W. Norton

Radford, Mike (2001): *Animal Welfare Law in Britain*, Open University Press

Raphael, D D (1990): *Problems of Political Philosophy*, second edition, Macmillan

Rawls, John (1972): *A Theory of Justice*, Clarendon Press

Rawls, John (2001): *Justice as Fairness: A Restatement*, ed Erin Kelly, Harvard University Press

Robinson, Dave and Groves, Judy (2003): *Introducing Political Philosophy*, Icon Books

Russell, Bertrand (1930): *The Conquest of Happiness*, Unwin

Ryan, Alan (1987): 'Introduction' to *Utilitarian and Other Essays: J S Mill and Jeremy Bentham*, ed Alan Ryan, Penguin

Ryder, Richard D (1970): *Speciesism*, Leaflet, Oxford

Ryder, Richard D (1975): *Victims of Science : The Use of Animals in Research*, Davis-Poynter, 1975

Ryder, Richard D (1989): *Animal Revolution : Changing Attitudes Towards Speciesism*, Blackwell

Ryder, Richard D (1989): *Animal Revolution: Changing Attitudes Towards Speciesism*, Basil Blackwell. Revised edition: Berg, 2000

Ryder, Richard D (1992a): 'Introduction' to *Animal Welfare and the Environment*, ed Richard D Ryder, Duckworth

Ryder, Richard D (1992b): 'Painism: The Ethics of Animal Rights' in *Animal Welfare and the Environment*, ed Richard D Ryder, Duckworth

Ryder, Richard D (1998): *Painism: The Ethics of Animal Experimentation*, Animals in Philosophy & Science, Holland

Ryder, Richard D (1998): *The Political Animal : The Conquest of Speciesism*, McFarland

Ryder, Richard D (2001): *Painism : A Modern Morality*, Opengate Press

Ryder, Richard D (2003): 'The Ethics of Pain', *The Philosopher's Magazine*, 23, 3rd Quarter 2003, pp 40–42

Ryder, Richard D (2004): 'Speciesism Revisited', *Think*, The Royal Institute of Philosophy, 6, Spring 2004, pp 83–92

Ryder, Richard D (2004): 'The Ethics of the Iraq War', *Think*, The Royal Institute of Philosophy, 8, Autumn 2004, pp 17-25

Sands Phillipe (2005): Personal Communication, July 2005

Sands, Philippe ed (2003): *From Nuremburg to the Hague : the Future of International Criminal Justice*, Cambridge University Press

Singer, Peter ed (1991): *A Companion to Ethics*, Blackwell Reference

Singer, Peter (2004): *The President of Good and Evil : Taking George W Bush Seriously*, Granta

Singer, Peter (2004): *The President of Good and Evil : Taking George W Bush Seriously*, Granta

Sterba, James P (2002): 'Liberalism and the Challenge of Communitarianism' in *The Blackwell Guide to Social and Political Philosophy*, ed Robert L. Simon, Blackwell

Stutzer, Alois and Frey, Bruno (2000): 'Happiness, Economy and Institutions', *Economic Journal*, October, 2000

Sutherland, Keith (2004): *The Party's Over: Blueprint for a Very English Revolution*, Imprint Academic

Taylor, Charles (1997): 'Nationalism and Modernity' in *The Morality of Nationalism*, ed Robert McKim and Jeff McMahan, Oxford University Press

Veenhoven, Ruut (2003): 'Happiness', *The Psychologist*, Vol. 16, No. 3, pp 128–129

Warren, Jane (2004): *Ali's Story*, Sunday Times, 4th April 2004

Webster, John (1994): *Animal Welfare : A Cool Eye Towards Eden*, Blackwell Science

Wolff, Jonathan (1996): *An Introduction to Political Philosophy*, Oxford University Press

Wood, Allen W. (2001): *Kant's Ethical Thought*, Cambridge University Press

Wright, Robert (1994): *The Moral Animal*, Abacus

Index

SOCIETAS: essays in political and cultural criticism

Public debate has been impoverished by two competing trends. On the one hand the trivialization of the media means that in-depth commentary has given way to the ten second soundbite. On the other hand the explosion of knowledge has increased specialization, and academic discourse is no longer comprehensible. As a result writing on politics and culture is either superficial or baffling.

This was not always so — especially for political debate. The high point of the English political pamphlet was the seventeenth century, when a number of small printer-publishers responded to the political ferment of the age with an outpouring of widely-accessible pamphlets and tracts. But in recent years the tradition of the political pamphlet has declined—with most publishers rejecting anything under 100,000 words. The result is that many a good idea ends up drowning in a sea of verbosity. However the introduction of the digital press makes it possible to re-create a more exciting age of publishing. *Societas* authors are all experts in their own field, but the essays are for a general audience. Each book can be read in an evening. The books are available retail at the price of £8.95/$17.90 each, or on bi-monthly subscription for only £5/$10. Details/updated schedule at **imprint-academic.com/societas**

EDITORIAL ADVISORY BOARD

IMPRINT ACADEMIC, PO Box 200, Exeter, EX5 5YX, UK
Tel: (0)1392 841600   Fax: (0)1392 841478   sandra@imprint.co.uk

SOCIETAS SUBSCRIPTION FORM

All Societas titles are available at the reduced price of £5.00 each to subscribers. To qualify for the reduced price, simply sign up for the current volume by direct debit. We will debit your account £5.00 when each book is despatched (every two months). Details of the next title will be supplied at the same time, so if you want to unsubscribe you can cancel the mandate.

☐ *Please register my **Societas** subscription, starting with the current volume. I would also like to order the following backlist titles (first two at only **£2.50** each, additional titles for £5.00)*

. . . .
. . . .
. . . .
. . . .

IMPRINT ACADEMIC — Instruction to your Bank or Building Society to pay by Direct Debit

Please fill in the form and send to Imprint Academic, PO Box 200, Exeter EX5 5YX

DIRECT Debit

To: The Manager — Bank/Building Society

Address

Postcode

Name(s) of Account Holder(s)

Branch Sort Code

Bank/Building Society account number

Originator's Identification Number

| 6 | 3 | 0 | 4 | 9 | 4 |

Reference

Instruction to your Bank or Building Society

Please pay Imprint Academic Direct Debits from the account detailed in this Instruction subject to the safeguards assured by the Direct Debit Guarantee. I understand that this instruction may remain with Imprint Academic and, if so, details will be passed electronically to my Bank/Building Society.

Signature(s)

Date

DDI5

Banks and Building Societies may not accept Direct Debit Instructions for some types of account

Name. . . . .

Address * . . . .

. . . .

Home telephone . . . . E-mail. . . . .

Send to: IMPRINT ACADEMIC, PO Box 200, Exeter EX5 5YX, UK
Tel: (0)1392 841600   Fax: (0)1392 841478   Email: sandra@imprint.co.uk